OPIUM

by James Barter

DRUG
EDUCATION
LIBRARY

LUCENT BOOKS

An imprint of Thomson Gale, a part of The Thomson Corporation

THOMSON
GALE

Detroit • New York • San Francisco • San Diego • New Haven, Conn.
Waterville, Maine • London • Munich

LIBRARY OF CONGRESS CATALOGING-IN-PUBLICATION DATA

Barter, James, 1946–
  Opium / by James Barter.
     p. cm. — (Drug education library)
  Includes bibliographical references and index.
  ISBN 1-59018-419-X (hardcover : alk. paper)
  1. Opium—Juvenile literature. I. Title. II. Series.
RM666.O6B34 2004
615'.7822—dc22

                                                      2004010688

Printed in the United States of America

Contents

Foreword

The development of drugs and drug use in America is a cultural paradox. On the one hand, strong, potentially dangerous drugs provide people with relief from numerous physical and psychological ailments. Sedatives like Valium counter the effects of anxiety; steroids treat severe burns, anemia, and some forms of cancer; morphine provides quick pain relief. On the other hand, many drugs (sedatives, steroids, and morphine among them) are consistently misused or abused. Millions of Americans struggle each year with drug addictions that overpower their ability to think and act rationally. Researchers often link drug abuse to criminal activity, traffic accidents, domestic violence, and suicide.

These harmful effects seem obvious today. Newspaper articles, medical papers, and scientific studies have highlighted the myriad problems drugs and drug use can cause. Yet, there was a time when many of the drugs now known to be harmful were actually believed to be beneficial. Cocaine, for example, was once hailed as a great cure, used to treat everything from nausea and weakness to colds and asthma. Developed in Europe during the 1880s, cocaine spread quickly to the United States where manufacturers made it the primary ingredient in such everyday substances as cough medicines, lozenges, and tonics. Likewise, heroin, an opium derivative, became a popular painkiller during the late nineteenth century. Doctors and patients flocked to American drugstores to buy heroin, described as the optimal cure for even the worst coughs and chest pains.

As more people began using these drugs, though, doctors, legislators, and the public at large began to realize that they were more damaging than beneficial. After years of using heroin as a painkiller, for example, patients began asking their doctors for larger and stronger doses. Cocaine users reported dangerous side effects, including hallucinations and wild mood shifts. As a result, the U.S. government initiated more stringent regulation of many powerful and addictive drugs, and in some cases outlawed them entirely.

A drug's legal status is not always indicative of how dangerous it is, however. Some drugs known to have harmful effects can be purchased legally in the United States and elsewhere. Nicotine, a key ingredient in cigarettes, is known to be highly addictive. In an effort to meet their bodies' demands for nicotine, smokers expose themselves to lung cancer, emphysema, and other life-threatening conditions. Despite these risks, nicotine is legal almost everywhere.

Other drugs that cannot be purchased or sold legally are the subject of much debate regarding their effects on physical and mental health. Marijuana, sometimes described as a gateway drug that leads users to other drugs, cannot legally be used, grown, or sold in this country. However, some research suggests that marijuana is neither addictive nor a gateway drug and that it might actually benefit cancer and AIDS patients by reducing pain and encouraging failing appetites. Despite these findings and occasional legislative attempts to change the drug's status, marijuana remains illegal.

The Drug Education Library examines the paradox of drugs and drug use in America by focusing on some of the most commonly used and abused drugs or categories of drugs available today. By discussing objectively the many types of drugs, their intended purposes, their effects (both planned and unplanned), and the controversies surrounding them, the books in this series provide readers with an understanding of the complex role drugs and drug use play in American society. Informative sidebars, annotated bibliographies, and organizations to contact lists highlight the text and provide young readers with many opportunities for further discussion and research.

Introduction

A Dark Paradise

Few sights in nature are more strikingly breathtaking than gently rolling fields blanketed by lavender, scarlet, white, and green opium poppies in full bloom. One of nature's most dramatic displays, their splashes of dazzling color are rivaled only by that of tropical fish cruising amid the coral reefs or parrot flocks gliding amid the tropical rain forest canopy.

However, the natural allure of the opium poppy in bloom masks a dark side unlike any other found in nature. Contained within the seedpod of the opium poppy is a gummy sap that bleeds from the surface when it is accidentally scratched or intentionally slit. Although the sap looks innocuous as it forms in droplets on the outer shell of the green pod, it becomes a dangerous narcotic once harvested and processed for millions of opium addicts who are dependent on its mystical yet tragic properties.

The consumption of opium, whether smoked, eaten, or injected, is marked by a euphoric rush, a warm feeling of relaxation, a sense of security and protection, and relief from hunger, tension, and physical pain. Millions of addicts around the world spend tens of billions of dollars a year to experience its tranquilizing pleasure. Worth more money per acre than any other crop in the

6

world, literally worth more than its weight in gold, the sap finds its way to the streets of all major cities.

Opium begins its journey in its raw state as a bitter, milky-brown, sticky sap. Only the sap of the poppy *Papaver somniferum* produces the intoxicating sticky juice. The genus name of this colorful plant comes from the Latin word for poppy, and the species name from the Latin word meaning "causing sleep." Its distinctive characteristic of inducing a dreamy, sleeplike trance is what differentiates it from dozens of other benign poppy species.

An Afghan farmer harvests opium, one of the world's most potent narcotics.

Flowing in the sap of the opium poppy is a narcotic that people have used and valued for five thousand years. Yet it was not until the advent of modern chemistry at the beginning of the nineteenth century that the principal ingredient, called *principium somniferum*, meaning "the basic ingredient inducing sleep," was isolated and identified as containing two powerful pain relievers. Referred to by doctors as analgesics, these pain relievers are morphine and codeine.

Once the chemistry of opium was understood, pharmacologists, chemists, botanists, and physicians experimented with the drug. They proclaimed it a panacea capable of treating a variety of painful maladies such as internal bleeding, broken bones, and even, it was hoped, cancer and alcoholism. So optimistic was the scientific community that it freely prescribed syrups and elixirs laced with opium to relieve the pain of the elderly and to quiet squalling babies.

By the end of the nineteenth century, Europeans and Americans of all ages and income groups were consuming doses of opium in pharmaceuticals as well as in a variety of commercial products sold in stores. Many more people were learning how to smoke the dried sap from Chinese laborers who had arrived in America in the mid-1800s to work in California's gold mines and to build the Transcontinental Railroad. Opium dens, hangouts where people met to smoke opium and then slump into a drowsy stupor, sprang up first in California and later in many cities across the American heartland.

As opium consumption in America increased, it became evident that something was terribly wrong. Occasional overdoses were

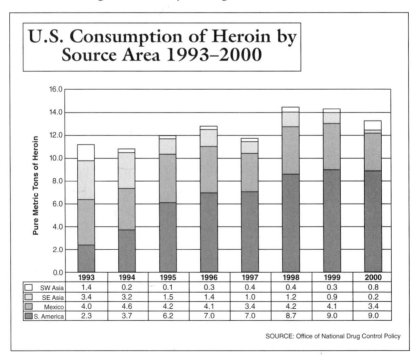

U.S. Consumption of Heroin by Source Area 1993–2000

Pure Metric Tons of Heroin

	1993	1994	1995	1996	1997	1998	1999	2000
SW Asia	1.4	0.2	0.1	0.3	0.4	0.4	0.3	0.8
SE Asia	3.4	3.2	1.5	1.4	1.0	1.2	0.9	0.2
Mexico	4.0	4.6	4.2	4.1	3.4	4.2	4.1	3.4
S. America	2.3	3.7	6.2	7.0	7.0	8.7	9.0	9.0

SOURCE: Office of National Drug Control Policy

costing users their lives, and the medical community was coming to grips with the startling discovery that opium was highly addictive. Addicts became more focused on finding and taking their drug than on their health and their families' well-being. Opium's ability to relieve pain and create a soothing mental state was making it one of the most widely used drugs.

Determined to battle the scourge of opium, America and other countries outlawed it at the beginning of the twentieth century. Desperately needing the drug, addicts became customers of major crime organizations that surfaced to provide an uninterrupted flow of the drug from Asian poppy fields to the streets of America at a hefty cost in terms of money, crime, and lives.

Today, as the twenty-first century moves forward, the opium problem remains. America's appetite for opium in its various forms, one of which is heroin, seems insatiable. Political and civic leaders have organized to try to free America from opium's grip but are divided on how best to do it. One faction has launched a war on the poppy fields in Asia, assuming that by destroying the source, America's problem will disappear. Another faction proposes that America can stop illicit trafficking only by confronting the demand for the drug at home. And yet a third smaller group doubts the bane can be eliminated.

None of these actions has resolved the war on opium. Its steady use is a major health and social problem. Opium continues to find its way to the streets of America regardless of the billions of dollars that are annually spent trying to stamp it out.

Chapter 1

A Strange and Mysterious Flower

Long ago, opium's strange and mysterious flower was enjoyed and celebrated by ancient civilizations. The plant was not perceived as having any medical, curative powers or deadly addictive properties. Instead, people believed that opium had mystical powers capable of inducing temporary happiness and a welcomed, trancelike slumber.

The earliest people to cultivate the opium poppy were the Sumerians, who occupied Mesopotamia in what is present-day Iraq. Five thousand years ago they referred to opium poppies as *hul gil*, meaning the "joy plant." Anthropologists believe that they probably discovered the plant's mysterious properties by observing the intoxicated behavior of cattle that had eaten the sap-filled pods. Out of curiosity, some Sumerians chewed the pods and experienced a calming bliss. Over time, the Sumerians gave away seeds and passed along claims about the plant's comforting effects to the Babylonians, who in turn passed it on to the Egyptians, who passed it on to the Greeks and Romans.

The Discovery of Drowsy Dreams

Some of the earliest references to opium's sleeplike trance come from clay tablets dating back to 2000 B.C. These tablets recommend calming fractious children with the juice of crushed poppies mixed with fly droppings; the mixture was ground into a pulp, forced through a cotton strainer, and administered orally for four days. It guaranteed peaceful, sleeping children.

One of the earliest literary references to the dulling and drowsy effects of opium can be found in the epics of Homer, a Greek writer from the ninth century B.C. In his book the *Iliad*, Homer mentions the use of opium by contingents of the Greek army that had gone to fight at the gates of Troy. Homer described a scene

Pictured on this cup dating from the fifth century B.C. is a scene from Homer's epic the Iliad, *which contains several references to opium use.*

Evidence of Ancient Opium Use

Archaeologists have discovered evidence of a thriving Bronze Age drug trade that supplied opium to ancient cultures throughout the eastern Mediterranean. They have evidence that opium was used thousands of years ago not only to relieve the pain of childbirth and disease but also as a recreational drug.

Ancient ceramic pots, most of them nearly identical in shape and about five inches long, have been found in tombs and settlements throughout the Middle East dating as far back as 1400 B.C. When turned upside down, these thin-necked pots with round bases resemble opium poppy pods. The round bases have two white markings, designs nearly identical to knife cuts made on poppy pods that allow the sap to ooze and be harvested.

Similar pots have also turned up in Egypt. Based on ancient Egyptian medical writings from the second millennium B.C., researchers believe opium was used during surgery and to treat aches, pains, and other ailments. From their study of Egyptian writings, archaeologists believe the opium was eaten rather than smoked.

Israel is another place where evidence of opium has been unearthed. In an archaeologically rich area of central Israel, a tomb from the late Roman period revealed the skeleton of a fourteen-year-old girl who died in childbirth around A.D. 390. On her stomach was a fleck of a burnt, brownish black substance that analysis identified as opium. The fleck was an extremely rare find, revealing that the drug was smoked, not eaten, in some early cultures.

Dating to about 1400 B.C., these vessels unearthed on the island of Cyprus were used as opium containers.

in which the Greek army was sitting around a campfire one evening: "The poppy which in the garden is weighted down by fruit and vernal showers, droops its heads to one side, saturated with lethal slumber."[1] Later in his second book the *Odyssey*, Homer warned Greek soldiers traveling in foreign lands against drinking opium-laced beverages because of their powers to "induce forgetfulness of pain and any sense of evil."[2]

Around 460 B.C., the Greek physician Hippocrates, one of the greatest Western figures in medicine, grew curious about the attributes of opium. He believed its strange effects could be explained scientifically, while most people of his time thought its properties were magical. Although he did not know why opium had an effect on people, he recognized its unusual analgesic powers and recommended it to patients suffering intense pain.

The Romans also knew of the drowsy effects of opium. In A.D. 77, Pedanius Dioscorides served in the Roman army as a physician and traveled widely. His enduring fame rests on his only known work, a compilation called *De Materia Medica (About Medical Material)*, describing about five hundred plants he had collected. In this work he recorded, "Poppies possess, as it were, a cooling power, therefore the leaves and head when boiled in water and drunk, bring sleep. The concoction is also drunk to remedy insomnia."[3]

Noting opium's power to induce wistful slumber, numb pain, and create a temporary state of bliss, the Arabs elected to introduce opium to the rest of the world. By the ninth century A.D., Arab traders sailing as far west as Spain and traveling in caravans as far north as Vienna were introducing Europe to the mysteries of this potent flower.

Opium and Europeans

Developing a vast network of contacts throughout Europe and the Middle East, Arab merchants traded in everything of value, from diamonds, ivory, silk, and coral to spices, coffee, and, most lucratively, opium. Opium was viewed as the perfect commodity for trade; it was valuable and highly compact, and when properly dried, it would not deteriorate. For the most part, opium was purchased in Europe during the Middle Ages to relieve pain and to ease the fear of warriors going into battle. It had developed a reputation as an effective drug to settle nerves and strengthen courage.

But Europe's upper crust—the only people who could regularly purchase the expensive drug—had other ideas of how to use it. For many of the elite, opium provided a pleasurable experience. In response to the soaring demand among the well heeled, opium was placed on every explorer's list of exotic merchandise to bring back home. Although Columbus's goal was to discover a route to India, he was asked to return with opium along with gold, spices, and a list of other prized items. His instructions were not unique; Ferdinand Magellan and Vasco da Gama were also asked to find opium in addition to dozens of other valued products.

As shipments of opium poured into Europe, claims about its capabilities became outrageous. Around 1520, a Swiss man by the name of Paracelsus claimed to have discovered a concoction made from opium, brandy, crushed pearls, a plant called henbane, and frog sperm that was capable of curing any disease. A contemporary named Oporinus said of Paracelsus's magical cure-all, "He boasted he could, with these pills, wake up the dead and certainly he proved this to be true for patients who appeared dead suddenly arose."[4] As this recipe and others spread throughout Europe, the pleasures of opium found their way into the merchant class and even into low-income families.

The Miracle of Laudanum

In 1680 the British physician Thomas Sydenham bottled opium and called it laudanum, from the Latin word meaning "worthy of praise." He did so partly in response to the demand for a convenient way to ingest opium, particularly for people suffering acute pain. His formula for the tasty and effective concoction was two ounces of opium, one ounce of saffron, and a dash of both cinnamon and clove, all dissolved in a pint of canary wine. To promote the latest of the opium elixirs, Sydenham proclaimed, "Among the remedies which it has pleased Almighty God to give to man to relieve his sufferings, none is so universal and so efficacious as opium."[5]

The popularity of laudanum swept across Europe. For some users it was a way to forget their problems, for others it relieved toothaches and stiff joints, and for an ever-growing group, it was nothing more than a soothing drink to be enjoyed among friends. The very poor also had any number of reasons to turn to laudanum for temporary emotional relief from their poverty and miserable living conditions in large, filthy industrial cities such as London.

By the mid-1700s, people of all classes would purchase a bottle on their way home to enjoy before the evening meal. Many wives expressed a preference for seeing their husbands consume a bottle of laudanum instead of a bottle of whiskey because the opium-laced drink induced a soothing sleep rather than a foul, obnoxious drunken stupor common with excessive alcohol consumption. As one wife remarked while standing over her drunken husband, "Ugh! It's shameful. Take laudanum instead, it's less disgusting."[6]

Poetic Praise

The people who sang the praises of opium's dreamlike state more than any other were a group of eighteenth- and nineteenth-century poets. Believing that opium stimulated their creativity, they wrote letters and composed poems praising its effects. Almost all of Britain's great eighteenth-century poets, such as Samuel Taylor Coleridge, Percy Bysshe Shelley, John Keats, and Lord Byron, intertwined their poetry with allusions to opium's mind-numbing pleasures.

Some eighteenth-century English poets like Samuel Taylor Coleridge alluded to opium use in their work.

Coleridge authored the well-known poem "Kubla Khan." Literary critic William Beal asserts that Coleridge "wrote a poem in a dream-like trance while under its spell; opium promotes vivid dreams and rich visual imagery as well as gentle euphoria."[7] According to Beal and other literary scholars, the imagery of "Kubla Khan" reflects an opium-induced trance as evidenced in the following lines of the poem:

In Xanadu did Kubla Khan

A stately pleasure-dome decree:

Where Alph, the sacred river, ran

Through caverns measureless to man

Down to a sunless sea

. . . .

I would build that dome in air,

That sunny dome! those caves of ice!

And all who heard should see them there,

. . . .

For he on honey-dew hath fed,

And drunk the milk of Paradise.[8]

Across the Atlantic in New York, William Blair cheerfully described his surreal experience with opium while attending a play:

I felt a strange sensation, totally unlike any thing I had ever felt before; a gradual creeping thrill, which in a few minutes occupied every part of my body, lulling to sleep . . . racking pain, producing a pleasing glow from head to foot, and inducing a sensation of dreamy exhilaration. . . . After I had been seated a few minutes, the nature of the excitement changed, and a "waking sleep" succeeded. The actors on the stage vanished; the stage itself lost its reality; and before my entranced sight magnificent halls stretched out in endless succession with gallery above gallery, while the roof was blazing with gems, like stars whose rays alone illumined the whole building, which was tinged with strange, gigantic figures, like the wild possessors of a lost globe. . . . I will not attempt farther to describe the magnificent vision which a little pill of "brown gum" had conjured up from the realm of ideal being. No words that I can command would do justice to its Titanian splendour and immensity.[9]

Literature praising opium did more to incite the public's curiosity about opium's euphoric effects than any other form of communication. Readers by the thousands obtained opium to experience it. While the scientific community still knew very little about its dangers, a few poets stepped forward to warn about opium's dark side. One was the French writer Charles-Pierre Baudelaire, who likened opium to a treacherous woman friend: "An old and terrible friend, and, alas! like them all, full of caresses and deceptions."[10]

Coleridge acknowledged opium's downside In "Kubla Khan" when he admitted,

> And all should cry, Beware! Beware!
>
> His flashing eyes, his floating hair!
>
> Weave a circle round him thrice,
>
> And close your eyes with holy dread.[11]

Regardless of these warnings, by the mid–nineteenth century, opium use was out of control. Its dark side had emerged.

Dreams Turn to Nightmares

The sweet euphoria initially enjoyed by so many soon turned sour. Pharmacists who sold bottles of laudanum reported seeing the same people buying it with increasing frequency and hearing them say they needed larger doses each evening. As laudanum and especially its key ingredient opium came under closer scrutiny, chemists and physicians recognized that many users were increasing their daily consumption rate.

Opium use in Europe was on the rise. Increasing numbers of laudanum users turned to the pure form of opium, which was often smoked, to satisfy their cravings. An anonymous writer in 1844 commented on opium's addictive quality: "Opium smoking is a sort of incline plane, down which he who ventures to slide a little way is tolerably sure to go to the bottom."[12]

As more users consumed opium, they needed larger and larger doses to experience the same numbing effect. The demand became

Confessions of an English Opium Eater

In 1821 the British writer Thomas De Quincey published his experiences with opium in the book *Confessions of an English Opium Eater*. His writings, the first to relate experiences of opium eating and addiction, were published at a time when opium was widely used for the relief of pain and before its addictive qualities were properly understood. It is a work that blends amusement with horror as the author undergoes the marvels of opium-induced dreams and the equally terrifying nightmares.

On the immediate and unexpected pleasures of his first opium experience De Quincey wrote:

> I arrived at my lodgings and lost not a moment in taking the quantity prescribed. I was necessarily ignorant of the whole art and mystery of opium-taking. . . . But I took it—and in an hour—oh, heavens! what a revulsion! what an upheaving, from its lowest depths, of inner spirit! what an apocalypse of the world within me! That my pains had vanished was now a trifle in my eyes: this negative effect was swallowed up in the immensity of those positive effects which had opened before me—in the abyss of divine enjoyment thus suddenly revealed. Here was a panacea, for all human woes; here was the secret of happiness, about which philosophers had disputed for so many ages, at once discovered: happiness might now be bought for a penny.

Later De Quincy described his addiction and then recovery:

> If opium-eating be a sensual pleasure, and if I am bound to confess that I have indulged in it to an excess, not yet recorded of any other man, it is no less true, that I have struggled against this fascinating enthrallment with a religious zeal, and have, at length, accomplished what I never yet heard attributed to any other man—have untwisted, almost to its final links the accursed chain which fettered [shackled] me.

Thomas De Quincey documented his opium addiction in Confessions of an English Opium Eater.

Throughout the nineteenth century, opium was widely available in pharmacies across Europe. Pictured here is a bustling scene in a pharmacy in Vienna.

so great that farmers in Europe attempted to cultivate the opium poppy, but it was to no avail, because the climate was too damp and cold. Instead, British traders purchased all they could from Turkey and Afghanistan for legal import to Europe and for export to China, where huge profits could be made trading it for tea, silk, and spices. Opium's addictive quality had been recognized by the Chinese government and its importation forbidden. The continuing illegal export of opium to China by the British triggered a two-phase war, aptly called the Opium Wars, between 1839 and 1842. They concluded with China being forced to accept opium and endure a growing addiction rate.

European physicians became alarmed at the increasing consumption, one noting how purchasers of laudanum hurried from the pharmacy shops with bottle in hand:

Back home, if he can wait that long, he gulps down his dose and sinks into profound sleep. But when he awakens it's to a state of nervous depression. A closer look shows us his jaundiced skin and his sunken eyes. His speech is thick, his lips are cracked, he's hunched over, and his limbs are like sticks.[13]

To maintain their high, many users preferred smoking opium. This created a distinct odor, drawing attention to its use. To avoid attracting too much attention, opium smokers sought the secretive confines of opium dens.

Opium Dens

Some of those who succumbed to addiction sought refuge and companionship in opium dens, which were privately owned establishments where opium users congregated to socialize, smoke opium, have a bite to eat, and fall asleep in a safe environment. Sprouting first throughout Asia and then Europe, they were brought to America by the Chinese and were common in many of America's large cities by the mid–nineteenth century. While the majority of patrons were men, women were welcomed and many enjoyed the atmosphere.

In 1877 a tourist to San Francisco accepted a tour of the city's Chinatown district and described her first experience inside an opium den:

We were led into a small, close, but clean room, filled with the fumes of burning opium—resembling those of roasting ground-nuts, and not disagreeable. A table stood in the centre, and around three sides ran a double tier of shelves and bunks, covered with matting and cushioned with pillows. Nearly all of these were filled with Chinamen, many of them containing two, with a little tray between them, holding a lamp and a horn box filled with black opium paste. But although every one was smoking, it was so early in the evening that the drug had not as yet wrought its full effect, and all were wide awake, talking, laughing, and apparently enjoying themselves hugely.[14]

Opium dens were commonly known by slang names such as "the joint," "hop joint," "lay-down joint," and "the dragon," while those frequenting them were called "pipes," "pipe-fiends," "hop-heads," and "yenshee boys." Opium pipes, which were sold

The First Opium War

Early in the nineteenth century, British consumption of Chinese tea was adversely affecting the British economy. Britain had nothing of interest to trade to the Chinese, who were given silver bullion in return for the tea. The drain of British silver quickly placed Britain at a serious trading disadvantage. To stop the silver drain, the British sought a commodity the Chinese would accept instead of silver.

At that time, British trading companies controlled opium production over the entire Indian subcontinent. British merchant ships were already smuggling some of the opium into China. Since opium was contraband, they paid no duties. The British began trading opium for tea and employed Chinese opium buyers to bribe Chinese officials to keep the illegal arrangement quiet.

In 1820, however, the Chinese government discovered the ruse and imposed the death penalty on Chinese importers. They opposed opium for economic and health reasons because of widespread addiction. Nonetheless, British naval officers and merchants built fortified floating opium warehouses offshore, and by 1830 opium trade to China reached an annual thirty thousand watertight chests, totaling more than 4.5 million pounds.

Opium addiction became a major social problem despite the Chinese government's attempts to enforce prohibition of the drug. After repeated attempts to stop its illegal importation, the Opium War erupted. In the spring of 1839 Chinese authorities at Canton confiscated and burned the entire opium supply. In response, the British occupied positions around Canton and fired cannons on the city.

The Chinese could not match the technological superiority of the British cannons. In 1842 China surrendered and agreed to the provisions of the Treaty of Nanking, which stated that the opium trade would continue and that Hong Kong would become a British colony.

British ships bombard the city of Canton during the Opium War.

in dens along with other paraphernalia, were referred to as "gongers," "dream sticks," "bamboos," and "saxophones," while the act of smoking opium was described as "being on the hip," "kicking the gong around," and "rolling the log."

Opium dens spawned an entire culture and attracted all classes of society. Dens appealing to the upper classes were ornately decorated and provided comfortable and safe accommodations. For a price, young boys were available as servants who would pack the pipes, light them, fetch food and water, and run errands for wealthy clients. After frequenters had slept off their opium-induced stupors, they either wandered home or indulged in another round of opium.

Addicts pose in a New York City opium den. Beginning in the late nineteenth century, privately owned opium dens became havens for habitual users.

Until this time, the medical profession had seen little reason to study scrupulously the effects of opium on the mind and body. But as addiction rates increased, a call was made to investigate opium's physiological and psychological effects.

Opium's Physiological Effects

Early studies of opium indicated it had significant physiological effects on the body. Most noticeable and of greatest concern to physicians was its depressing effect on the heart and respiration. Clinical observations detected a slower respiration and heartbeat within minutes of ingestion, a suppression of the cough reflex, and constriction of the smooth muscles of the intestinal tract, causing constipation.

Physicians recognized that part of the sleepy, blissful experiences reported by patients was the result of a lowered respiration and heart rate. Oxygen shortages associated with slow respiration were known to produce a light-headed sensation, causing a person to become disoriented, forgetful, and seemingly unaware of his or her surroundings. Coupled with a decreased heart rate, this robbed the brain of oxygen-rich blood, causing drowsiness in all cases and even death in some.

Early physicians also identified a decline of opium smokers' general health. Using opium regularly, especially smoking it, caused a loss of appetite and led to severe weight loss. Physicians noted the abnormal skin colors of long-term smokers caused by poor nutrition and a lack of oxygen, which is necessary for healthy skin and internal organs.

Physicians also learned that the method of consumption had an effect on the body. Early experimentation confirmed that people who smoked opium reacted to the drug faster and more intensely than those who consumed it orally. What physicians learned from these experiments was that the smoke of opium entered the lungs, where it was immediately absorbed through the lung membrane along with oxygen and then carried by the blood to the brain within a matter of seconds. Laudanum, on the other hand, arrived at the brain much more slowly because it first passed into the

Smoking Opium

Prior to the invention of hypodermic needles, the most potent way to consume opium was to smoke it. Smoking still occurs today throughout Asia, although injecting it is more common in Western nations.

Traditionally, opium was smoked in a pipe specifically designed for opium. The design of each pipe always included two standard features: a very small bowl at one end and a long neck through which the smoke was drawn. The bowl was small because two or three inhales of a piece of opium the size of a pea were sufficient to intoxicate the smoker. The long neck, between eighteen and thirty inches, was sufficiently long to cool the hot smoke as it was drawn from the bowl. Nearly all opium pipes were long, but they came in a variety of shapes. Many had elegant curves and were made from a variety of exotic woods and animal bone. Others were expensive works of art purchased at high prices by those who could afford the status symbol of an artistically crafted pipe.

stomach and then through the intestines, where it was exchanged into the bloodstream along with food before being carried to the brain. Very early experiments in which dogs were injected with a liquid solution of opium indicated that injection created an even more intense high because the opium is more concentrated in the brain than when it is smoked or ingested.

In addition to looking at the physiological effects of opium, physicians studied the psychological changes in opium users. These generally consisted of an initial pleasurable heightening of the senses and feelings of well-being followed by a lapse into depression, causing changes in thinking and behavior.

Psychological Effects

One of the earliest Europeans to describe the psychological effects of opium was the Frenchman Jean Chardin, who visited Persia in 1720. In his book *Descriptions of Persia*, he explained that opium was eaten in pill form, about the size of a pea, and that Persian royalty enjoyed it as an alternative to wine. In his book, Chardin noted the bliss associated with opium as well as the unpleasant withdrawal that occurs soon after the effects of opium wear off:

It entertains their Fancies with pleasant Visions and a kind of Rapture; they grow Merry, then Swoon away with Laughing and say and do a thousand Extravagant Things. After the Operation is over, the Body grows Cold, Pensive, and Heavy, and remains in that manner, Indolent and Drowsy, until the Pill is repeated.[15]

Many writers of the late eighteenth and early nineteenth centuries wrote about the rapturous effects that opium had on their minds. The British novelist Edward George Bulwer-Lytton, who regularly smoked opium, suggested that opium enhanced his intellectual well-being: "A pipe is the fountain of contemplation, the source of pleasure, the companion of the wise; and the man who smokes, thinks like a philosopher and acts like a Samaritan."[16] The English poet Charles Lamb indicated in verse in 1805 his pleasures with opium: "May my last breath be drawn through a pipe, and exhaled in a jest."[17]

The small number of physicians who studied the effects of opium determined that more research was needed. The motive at the time was not so much a concern to stop its use as it was to determine how the mysterious drug might better serve medical science.

Chapter 2

The Search for Better Health

The history of medicine is the history of a quest for better and more certain means to treat disease and pain. Modern physicians readily admit that until the early 1800s science played only a minor role in curing diseases. Before then, thousands of patients suffering from a variety of diseases were treated with baseless cures often dating back to the Middle Ages. Physicians recommended unscientific and often ineffectual treatments such as purging the body by inducing vomiting and diarrhea, removing "bad blood" by placing leeches on the patient's skin, and "balancing the body" with a variety of traditional herbal remedies.

In the context of this historical backdrop, the discovery of opium's analgesic and possibly curative properties caused optimism to soar within the medical community. Finding cures for many common yet life-threatening diseases was suddenly a real possibility. The few people who studied and wrote about opium believed that it had the potential to become the panacea drug of the nineteenth century. As research and time pushed forward, scientists committed their energies to understanding opium's effects on the mind and body. Slowly and shakily at first, a solid body of medical knowledge emerged by the end of the twentieth century.

Early Medical Applications

By the mid–nineteenth century, many physicians viewed opium as a medicine rather than as a recreational drug. Opium had become an accepted part of medical practices, even though British and American physicians had only a rudimentary understanding of its effects on the body. Illustrative of the confusion of the time was a debate over whether the drug possessed stimulant or sedative properties. It was not until the twentieth century that opium was correctly identified as a sedative.

Of greatest interest was the medical application of opium as an analgesic during and following surgery and for patients with painful yet inoperable diseases such as advanced cancers. Other rudimentary analgesics and anesthetics—substances that totally block pain temporarily—nearly killed the patient in order to be effective. Opium, however, became prized by physicians because in controlled doses it alleviated pain while allowing the patient's body and mind to function properly.

Opium was used as an anesthetic during surgery. The science of anesthesia would not originate until the early twentieth century, when gases such as ether and chloroform were discovered. Until their discovery, the sedative effects of opium, which was administered in higher doses for surgery than for pain relief, partially worked to anesthetize patients. Great care was given in determining the dosage, because physicians understood that an overdose would suppress respiration and kill the patient.

Opium as an anesthetic and analgesic was heralded as one of the greatest medical breakthroughs of its time. In the 1850s, medical research facilities conducted extensive chemical analysis on the content of opium sap and discovered a variety of compounds responsible for reducing pain. Doctors and pharmacologists recognized that millions of lives could be saved using opium to sedate patients during surgeries because longer and more complicated surgical procedures would be possible. Within ten years, compounds containing opium were being manufactured into pills for medical use. In the 1860s, during the Civil War, Union army physicians used opium during surgeries for amputations, internal

In this nineteenth-century illustration, a physician administers opium to a patient before surgery.

wounds, and shrapnel removal. They also issued an estimated 10 million opium pills to soldiers recovering from surgeries.

Following the war, doctors heard about opium's success on the battlefield and envisioned more applications. Stories about opium's ability to relieve pain without debilitating the patient attracted obstetricians concerned with the pain of childbirth. Women welcomed the relief they experienced with opium while delivering healthy babies. Opium also proved helpful in relieving the intense pain of patients suffering from third-degree burns or undergoing cleft palate operations, nose and throat surgery, or tooth extractions. Oncologists prescribed it to relieve the severe pain experienced by patients with incurable forms of cancer, and cardiologists used it on patients suffering from heart disease because of opium's ability to calm and quiet victims.

Researchers experimenting with opium further discovered that the drug caused constrictions of the intestinal lining, reducing fluid loss associated with diarrhea. Diarrhea, which contributed to a victim's death by causing acute dehydration and loss of vital chemicals, was a symptom of such deadly diseases as malaria, typhoid fever, dysentery, and yellow fever.

Doctors soon were hopeful that opium pills might cure a wider range of diseases. They prescribed opium for anemia, insanity, tetanus, and a variety of complaints associated with pregnancy. Physicians were so pleased with opium that they referred to it as "GOM," meaning "God's own medicine."

During the Civil War, opium was widely used as a painkiller. Here, a nurse tends to the needs of two wounded Union soldiers.

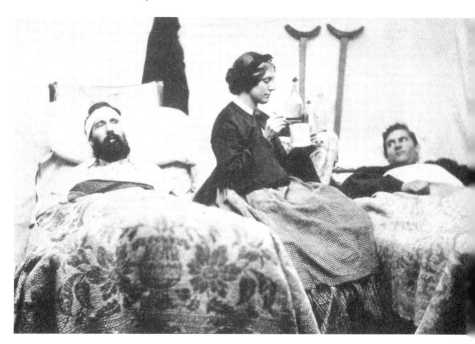

Commercial Value

Shortly after physicians discovered the medicinal value of opium, pharmaceutical companies saw it as a gold mine. Bypassing doctors, they marketed syrups and powders laced with opium directly to American families to soothe everyday aches and pains. By the early 1900s, use of opium in commercialized products exceeded its medical use.

One of the most popular commercial items were opium-fortified teething powders used to tranquilize crying babies who were cutting new teeth. Prior to the availability of opium, all teething remedies were alcohol based; ignorant of any possible side effects of opium, mothers gladly substituted it for alcohol. Opium was so successful that pharmaceutical companies sold it as a cure for other childhood medical problems, from earaches and bedwetting to measles, cholera, and diarrhea. Door-to-door salesmen working for Mother Bailey's Quieting Syrup, Mrs. Winslow's Soothing Syrup, and Ayer's Cherry Pectoral sold medicines spiked with 10 percent opium. If mothers were not home, samples were left on doorsteps. The confectionary business soon joined in, adding small dosages of opium, about 5 percent, to candy and sugary carbonated children's drinks.

Adults also enjoyed opium's effects on a variety of aches and pains. Several beverage manufacturers concocted a mix of opium and alcohol and marketed it as a healthful drink. They publicized their health drinks as capable of calming nerves, curing common aches and pains, and imparting a general sense of well-being. At the end of the nineteenth century, a variety of opium-based medicines were cheaper than a bottle of gin or whiskey. For this reason, drinks aimed at adult consumers, such as Battley's Sedative Solution, Dalby's Carminative, and Godfrey's Cordial, became popular drinks for the working class as well as for high society.

Enter the Snake-Oil Salesmen

Once the medical profession had touted the legitimate value of opium for surgery and pharmaceutical companies had filled medicine cabinets with opium-based medicine, charlatans looking to make a quick buck saw their opportunity to jump on the opium

A nineteenth-century poster advertises one of the many opium-based tonics peddled by traveling salesmen.

bandwagon. Although these hucksters, often referred to as snake-oil salesmen, had little understanding of medicine, they represented the only medical advice and supply of medicine available to many Americans farming remote parts of the Great Plains behind horse-drawn plows.

Between 1880 and 1920, these opium-laced cure-alls, which were unmitigated shams, were bottled by traveling salesmen and sold to the gullible public. These charlatans traveled from town to town, attending state and county fairs across rural America. They set up shop in the backs of their wagons and trucks and falsely claimed that their medicines were patented and capable of curing dozens of common disorders. The labels on the back of the bottles promised that the contents could cure everything from cancer to measles and even marriage problems. In most cases the contents of the bottle had little curative value and in some cases even inflicted harm. In all cases, it was opium's tranquilizing effect that soothed the buyers' pains and fooled them into thinking they were getting well.

Successful salesmen were great actors, not great men of medicine. Many wore flamboyant theatrical costumes and adopted colorful names, such as William Kroeger, the Priest-Healer of Epiphany, South Dakota; the Texas Outlaw Medicine Men; Indian John; and Daring Dr. Sofie. Guarantees of pain relief and better health accompanied every sale, and the crowds were enticed to purchase by shills planted in the audience who would step forward to testify to their improved health as a result of the bottled medicine.

A traveling salesman pitches a tonic in this movie still. Such salesmen often employed ruses to dupe the public into purchasing their tonics.

The men selling opium-laced potions were successful because a couple of swigs from the bottle gave the patient comfort for a few hours. But as the analgesic effect of the opium wore off, whatever pain and discomfort that had prompted the buyer to purchase the tonic returned. Swallowing more of the bottle's contents caused the dazed state to return, much to the relief and satisfaction of the buyer. The labels on most bottles advertised that the contents would bring relief, cause no harm, and save money over more expensive doctor visits. One such label from the 1890s carried this poem:

> Never causing any sore,
>
> Causing blood to run or pour,
>
> A bottle costs you fifty cents,
>
> Saving pain and great expense.[18]

The Dark Side of Paradise

The reckless proliferation of opium-based medicines, snake oils, and palliative elixirs during the late 1800s and early 1900s gradually exposed users to the dark side of opium. Those hawking opium tonics tended to focus on the relief and pleasure that they provide, but late-nineteenth- and early-twentieth-century doctors had begun to detect and document the agony of those who took increasing doses and some who took too much and died from overdosing. Widespread use of opium in America, its ability to reduce pain yet not cure any disease, and the unpleasant and even painful symptoms that occurred when people tried to stop using the drug prompted the medical profession to upgrade its concern about the effects of opium from worry to fear.

Despite disturbing new discoveries and conflicting views, many Americans consumed opium and most physicians continued to prescribe it because medical knowledge of the drug's properties was scanty and unreliable. Only a smattering of doctors realized that opium use was a growing problem, and few understood why it was addictive or why chronic users experienced withdrawal symptoms when they tried to discontinue or diminish dosages.

At this juncture, the dark side of paradise was beginning to emerge in small medical circles, even though the citizenry continued to believe, mistakenly, that opium was beneficial. Laudanum was freely dispensed to relieve pain and to cure a host of emotional and psychological disorders. Historian Alethea Hayter points out that in the late nineteenth century, "Most doctors and patients still thought of opium not as a dangerous addictive drug but mainly as a useful analgesic and tranquillizer of which every household should have a supply, for minor ailments and nervous crises of all kinds, much as aspirin is used today."[19]

Gradually doctors recognized that the core problem with opium use was addiction, the apparent uncontrollable need to be constantly under the drug's influence. To counter what was an obviously growing problem, doctors and pharmacists took on the daunting task of studying and attempting to control opium addiction.

Opium Addiction

Conservative estimates from the early 1900s reported that the United States had four hundred thousand addicts. Initial research established that addiction may take only two to three months to develop, depending upon the method of ingestion; injection was the fastest route to addiction, followed by smoking and then oral consumption.

The medical profession discovered that opium addiction has three stages. The first stage surfaces after some period of regular use when a person requires elevated dosages to produce the same physiological effect. They labeled this stage *tolerance*, a term that reflects the body's ability to tolerate the drug over time, which means the drug's effects diminish. In the case of opium, the user's body gradually stops experiencing pain relief and the mind ceases to experience euphoric drowsiness when small amounts of opium are consumed.

Chemists discovered two mechanisms for tolerance: metabolic and neurochemical. In metabolic tolerance, the body becomes more efficient at metabolizing the opium and thus the analgesic

Treatment Episodes of Opiates Abuse in the United States 1992 – 2002

Primary Substance	Total Opiates	Heroin	Other opiates/synthetics	Non-RX methadone	Other opiates/synthetics
1992	182,876	168,321	13,555	1,198	12,357
1993	206,839	192,816	14,023	1,279	12,744
1994	227,757	212,311	15,446	1,393	14,053
1995	236,748	220,972	15,776	1,274	14,502
1996	232,934	216,810	16,124	1,255	14,869
1997	251,417	235,143	16,274	1,209	15,065
1998	267,010	247,069	19,941	1,576	18,365
1999	280,345	257,340	23,005	1,602	21,403
2000	302,500	273,446	29,054	1,854	27,200
2001	316,373	277,911	38,361	2,037	36,425
2002	331,272	285,667	45,605	2,504	43,101

SOURCE: Office of Applied Studies, Substance Abuse and Mental Health Services Administration, Treatment Episode Data Set (TEDS)—3.1.04.

effects diminish. During the development of neurochemical tolerance, a realignment in the brain causes permanent changes to brain cells. Eventually the relaxing, sleepy effect of opium is partially blocked. Biochemists explain that when opium dosage is elevated, fewer receptors are needed to absorb the drug. When the number of receptors in the brain declines, the effects of opium are blocked. Later, however, when the amount of opium in the body dramatically declines, there are no longer enough receptors for the brain to function normally.

The discovery of the tolerance stage led to the discovery of the second stage of addiction. During this stage, the opium addict eventually needs more opium to sustain the desired effect. In time, either the amount or frequency of dosages are increased to provide the same relief initially experienced. Typical addicts begin by smoking opium once or twice a week but eventually increase the frequency to four to six times a day to maintain a constant trance.

During the third stage, both physical and psychological dependency occur. Regular opium use renders the addict dependent on

The Opium Rush

When opium is injected or smoked, the peak effects are usually felt within the first few minutes, a sensation known as a rush. The rush, which lasts only two to five minutes, is caused when a surge of opium alkaloids bathe the brain before the opium is distributed and diluted by the bloodstream, filtered out by the kidneys, and converted into other chemical forms that can be metabolized by the body.

The intensity of the rush is a function of how much opium is taken and how rapidly the drug enters the brain and binds to the brain's natural receptors. The rush is usually accompanied by a warm flushing of the skin, a dry mouth, and a heavy, sleepy feeling in the extremities. When the dose is unusually high, a feeling of nausea along with vomiting and severe itching.

For many addicts, the rush is more addictive than the three- or four-hour high that follows it. The intensity of the rush has been described as a pleasurable explosion in the brain, intense sexual pleasure, a state of uncontrollable laughter, and a spiritual experience. In general, addicts report a profound sense of satisfaction, as though all needs have been fulfilled. There is also a state of mild dizziness and a sense of distance or apathy from whatever problems or concerns the user might have.

A Pakistani man sits dazed as the opium he has smoked enters his bloodstream.

the drug in order to maintain a satisfactory level of physical and emotional pleasure. The absence of opium triggers physical withdrawal symptoms that resemble an extreme case of the flu accompanied by severe headaches, vomiting, uncontrolled trembling, and a drop in body temperature. Emotional withdrawal symptoms are characterized by an intense desire for the drug, a feeling that the drug is necessary for happiness and contentment and a fear of not having a supply of it. For some addicts, withdrawal also includes nightmares; hallucinations, including sightings of imaginary objects and people while awake; and profound depression that can lead to suicide attempts.

Around 1910, the scientific community was alarmed. It now regarded opium as one of the most highly addictive and debilitating substances known. Chemists and pharmacologists committed enormous resources to discover what was in the opium sap that imparted its addictive quality.

The Chemistry of Opium

The secret of opium's mystical and medicinal properties lay deep within the sticky, milky substance that drips from the incised pods. The first person to investigate the chemical components of raw opium was Wilhelm Sertürner, a German chemist who in 1805 crudely decomposed raw opium paste into a handful of components, one of which was a collection of alkaloids, organic chemical compounds. Sertürner identified a few of the alkaloids that produced opium's analgesic affects, along with many that did not. The alkaloid that was most prevalent he aptly named morphine after the Greek god of dreams, Morpheus.

Twentieth-century chemists, who had the advantage of more sophisticated procedures and equipment, tested raw opium and discovered that its pasty substance was more complex than Sertürner had realized. They discovered sugars, proteins, fats, water, meconic acid, plant wax, latex, gums, ammonia, sulphuric and lactic acids, and many more alkaloids than Sertürner had identified. They identified fifty or so alkaloids, measured their concentrations, and were most intrigued by four: morphine (which constitutes 10 to 15 percent of raw opium), noscapine (4 to 8 percent), codeine (1 to 3 percent), and papaverine (1 to 3 percent). Researchers determined that these four alkaloids were collectively responsible for opium's analgesic value. (One of the alkaloids, morphine, was later used to create the synthetic drug heroin.)

Physicians were excited by these revolutionary discoveries about these alkaloids and by the possibility of using opium to cure diseases such as alcoholism. Of greater interest to the general medical community, however, were the causes of opium's analgesic effects and the intoxicating dreamlike state enjoyed by all who took it. To understand how opium produced these desirable effects, chemists sought the assistance of neurologists, researchers who specialize in the functions of the brain.

Opium and the Brain

In 1972 a group of chemists and neurologists, headed by Dr. Solomon Snyder of Johns Hopkins University, made a puzzling discovery that would illuminate scientists' understanding of how opium influences the brain. They found that the human brain's billions of neurons had specific receptor sites—places where chemicals of various types are absorbed—that have molecular structures very similar to those of several of the opium alkaloids. Because of the molecular similarity of the receptors and the alkaloids, the two combine when they make contact, much like two pieces of a jigsaw puzzle snap together. When they lock up, a process biochemists call binding, the neurons absorb the alkaloids.

This discovery about opium alkaloid absorption suggested to researchers that the brain had evolved to bind with opium alkaloids. But then there was the obvious question of why the human brain would need a receptor for a plant. Further research revealed a likely answer to the question. Dr. Snyder and his team made the startling discovery that the molecular structure of opium is remarkably similar to compounds naturally produced in humans called endorphins. Endorphins are chemicals responsible for pain relief, happiness, and relaxation. Some of the opium alkaloids, particularly morphine and codeine, mimic high levels of endorphins, relieving pain and producing a heightened state of well-being.

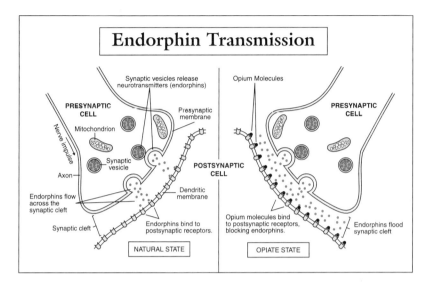

The Role of Endorphins

Pharmacologists performed additional research to understand the biochemical mechanism that allows opium and endorphins to produces their pleasurable effects. An endorphin is a special chemical called a neurotransmitter, which has the job of transmitting electrical messages from one neuron to the next. Endorphins flow from neurons into the synapses, the tiny spaces between neurons, to form temporary bridges that carry electrical signals across the synapses. Normally, after a neuron has transmitted its signal to the next neuron, the endorphin exits the synapse, returning to the same neuron that released it in a recycling process called reuptake. However, if opium is present while an electrical signal is taking place, scientists believe the opium blocks the reuptake process, resulting in a buildup of endorphins in the synapse. As the buildup of the endorphin neurotransmitter continues, any pain or discomfort experienced by the user is relieved and a peaceful dreamy sensation is experienced.

According to Dr. Snyder, "Like an evil twin, the opium molecules lock onto the endorphin-receptor sites on nerve endings in the brain and begin the succession of events that leads to euphoria or analgesia. This imposter is more powerful than the body's

Opium Withdrawal

Opium withdrawal is the emotional depression and physical distress that sets in three to four hours after a user experiences the euphoria of the opium rush. Withdrawal occurs because the body and mind have adapted to the presence of the drug and withdrawal symptoms arise when use is reduced or stopped.

Initial withdrawal produces a craving for more opium, restlessness, muscle and bone pain, insomnia, diarrhea, vomiting, sneezing, a runny nose, and chills with goose bumps—the last of which gave rise to the term "cold turkey," meaning an abrupt abstinence. Muscle spasms, produce kicking movements, from which came the term "kicking the habit," meaning eliminating the habit. Major withdrawal symptoms peak between two and three days after the last dose and subside after about a week. Sudden withdrawals by heavily dependent users who are in poor health are occasionally fatal if the addicts fail to eat a healthy, balanced diet.

Secondary withdrawal symptoms can occur for weeks and months thereafter. These include chronic depression, anxiety, insomnia, loss of appetite, periods of agitation, and a continued craving for the drug. In some cases, the severity of depression leads to death from suicide. Addicts experiencing withdrawal may walk across congested freeways, fall or jump from balconies, or drive their cars into concrete abutments. In spite of the struggle for addicts, opium withdrawal is considered within the medical profession to be much less dangerous and difficult than alcohol or nicotine withdrawal.

Recovering opium addicts remain hospitalized in a Polish detox clinic to help them cope with withdrawal symptoms.

own endorphins because the organism can not actually control how much of the feel-good chemical hits the brain."[20]

When the opium wears off, however, the reuptake process begins and the endorphin levels drop, causing the euphoria to disappear as fast as it appeared. The euphoria is replaced by depression and the user experiences irritability, fatigue, and an intense craving for more of the drug to escape the depression.

Different opium alkaloids bind with different neurotransmitters. Some bind in the respiratory center of the brain, causing breathing to slow. When opium addicts overdose, the overload of those opium alkaloids that bind with respiratory receptors causes breathing to come to a complete halt. Other opium alkaloids bind with an area of the brain that inhibits sensitivity to the impulse to cough, while still others bind with receptors in the brain's vomiting center, inducing excessive nausea and vomiting.

The discovery of the brain's neurotransmitters and their ability to bind with opium alkaloids was revolutionary. Regardless of the useful scientific information it yielded, it convinced a majority of Americans and their political and spiritual leaders that all opium-based drugs should be confiscated and destroyed. Although opium is illegal today, such an objective is still a difficult undertaking, because the international opium alliance that produces and distributes opium throughout the world is a massive multibillion-dollar enterprise that resists efforts to eliminate it.

Chapter 3

The Opium Alliance

The opium route—beginning in the poppy fields of Asia and ending thousands of miles away in hundreds of American and European cities—was built and operated by an illicit and sometimes violent opium alliance. America's opium addicts are the final link in a chain of secret criminal transactions that begin in the fields, pass through clandestine processing and packaging laboratories, and enter the United States through a maze of international smuggling routes. This highly coordinated, complex opium alliance is the world's most profitable criminal enterprise, involving millions of peasant farmers, thousands of corrupt government officials, disciplined criminal cartels, and organized American crime syndicates. Most of those involved in the opium route will never meet.

This underground industry is largely controlled by cartels. The Drug Enforcement Administration (DEA) estimates that 90 percent of the opium sold around the world is done so under the direction of about thirty cartels, which are well-organized and well-financed family-run businesses that control opium's production, distribution, and prices.

All nations involved in the opium trade repudiate the drug, yet the business flourishes. The success of this multinational, multibillion-dollar-a-year partnership begins with simple ingredients: earth, water, sunshine, and a tiny seed half the size of an ant's head. Many geographical locations are well suited for the opium poppy, but none more so than two locations in Asia whose names reflect the value of the crop grown there: the Golden Triangle and the Golden Crescent.

The Golden Triangle is a narrow, triangular-shaped band of mountains that stretches along the southern rim of the Asian landmass encompassing Thailand, Myanmar (formerly Burma), and Laos in Southeast Asia. Myanmar is the leading producer of opium within the triangle, according to the United Nations Drug Control Program (UNDCP).

The name Golden Crescent describes the opium poppy fields lining the crescent-shaped sweep of mountains running through Afghanistan, Iran, and Pakistan in southwest Asia. Estimates by the UNDCP indicate that this region is responsible for up to 80 percent of the world's opium production and that Afghanistan leads all nations in production. In 1999, according to field and

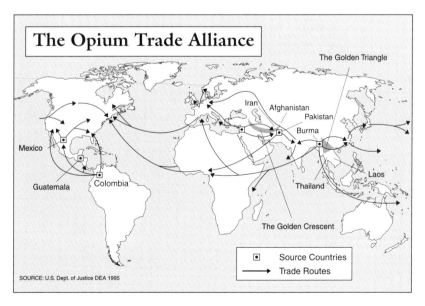

satellite surveys performed by the UNDCP, Afghanistan produced an estimated forty-five hundred tons of the drug. Recently Mexico, Colombia, and Peru joined these two leading opium centers as opium-growing nations.

Poppies provide a comfortable living for opium farmers, but growing and harvesting an illegal crop for export requires greater sophistication and organization than they can provide. Coordinating the efforts of so many individuals requires the financial and organizational muscle of opium cartels.

Opium Cartels

Opium cartels are run and organized like any large corporation. At the top are the presidents, referred to by a variety of names such as bosses, masters, warlords, and drug barons. Wealthy, politically influential within local governments, and known to use violence, they oversee a cadre of midlevel and low-level managers, accountants, attorneys, security forces, and hundreds of thousands of general field workers, all of whom support the growing, manufacturing, distributing, and selling of opium.

The success of cartels is closely tied to corruption. Much of their money is spent on bribes to silence law enforcement officers and politicians and to keep newspaper owners from publishing stories illuminating their corrupt practices. If bribery fails, cartels have other ways to achieve their objectives. Threats and occasional assassinations are not unusual. Another successful tactic is to spend drug money on the election campaigns of friends and family members who, if elected, will protect the cartels' illegal activities. On rare occasions, when all these measures fail and a senior cartel member is arrested, bosses hire lawyers to fight convictions and jail sentences. So many politicians and judges are controlled by the cartels that justice is rarely carried out. According to Don Ferrarone, a DEA agent in Myanmar, most drug lords avoid jail by one tactic or another:

> [Government] organizations that were supposed to be out there combating this problem had a very cozy, tight relationship [with drug bosses]. In fact, over twenty years we know of nobody of any significance that went to

Does Anyone Understand the Opium Alliance?

The illegal and secretive activities of members of the opium alliance make it difficult for law enforcement to understand its operations. Almost all data about the opium alliance comes from either the U.S. government or the United Nations. Critics of programs to eradicate opium poppies are skeptical about U.S. and UN figures citing decreases in opium production throughout the Golden Triangle and the Golden Crescent. Critics allege that opium plantation owners lie about the extent of their fields and have shifted field locations to avoid satellite and aerial detection. Many fields have been moved away from roads used by authorities and international observers.

In the article "Officials, Critics Clash over Myanmar Opium Questions," one critic, interviewed in northern Thailand, said, "No one knows how much opium is being grown in Myanmar," adding, "the U.N. and U.S. surveys have no validity." Verifying an observation frequently made by government critics, the same article claimed, "The Myanmar government periodically burns opium for visiting reporters, but it is all for show. We also saw a field destroyed for television cameras, but only after the sap had been harvested."

At the heart of the opium controversy and misunderstanding is money; money made in the production and sale of opium and money made by agreeing not to produce and sell opium. In this sense, opium farmers and government officials in poppy-growing nations profit both from producing it and from promising not to produce it. Critics charge that poppy growers and government officials in poppy-growing nations falsely report reductions in opium production because by doing so they will receive more financial aid from the United States, Great Britain, and the United Nations.

jail. A few would get arrested but they were right back out again. There was a very efficient penetration of certain politicians in critical locations that were simply getting their palms greased.[21]

The success of cartels is also closely tied to violence. Cartels are protected and maintained by an arsenal of weapons familiar to professional armies. These arsenals consist of the usual small arms as well as heavy artillery, including rocket-propelled grenade launchers, 105-millimeter mortars, and even surface-to-air missiles for use against government helicopters. Violence is also used against many civilians not associated with the opium trade. Cartel armies invading a rival's opium fields often encounter mined footpaths intended to blow up an invading squad. To prevent losing their men to land mines, invaders entering unknown territory coerce local villagers to act as human mine detectors by forcing them to walk in front of the troops.

The Opium Bosses

At the head of the opium cartels are the bosses. These positions are kept within families and handed down from father to son. Cartel bosses typically remain detached from the opium fields and distribution routes. For reasons of security, most conduct business behind the walls of well-guarded estates rivaling those of the world's wealthiest people. Cartel bosses travel in expensive imported luxury cars on their way to the finest restaurants and re-

Soldiers in the Shan United Army, Myanmar opium king Khun Sa's massive army, stand at attention.

sorts. Many own multiple homes in the world's major cities that serve as vacation sites and as safe havens should they ever need to take refuge from authorities.

Although this opulent lifestyle appears glamorous, it has its dark side. Cartel bosses have many enemies within rival cartels and are subject to arrest by international law enforcement agencies. Wherever the bosses or their family members go, armed bodyguards accompany them, and their cars are custom fitted with armor to withstand gunshots and bomb blasts. To achieve the same level of security in their estates, high walls and electronic monitoring devices deter attacks.

The most dominant opium boss for the past thirty years has been Khun Sa, who heads the Shan United Army in Myanmar. Khun Sa is internationally recognized as the opium king. He boasts an army between twenty and twenty-five thousand soldiers, who protect the fields and trade routes and provide security for himself, his family, and his associates. At the height of Khun Sa's dominance in the mid-1990s, his share of the Myanmar opium market was estimated at 80 percent, or more than $1 billion annually. Don Ferrarone made the following observation about Khun Sa's life in a 1996 interview:

The man is first and foremost a drug trafficker. He had a lot of skirmishes with other insurgent ethnic and trafficking organizations in the Shan State. These battles were [fought by] folks with M16's and AK47's and grenade launchers and artillery and mortars and the whole nine yards. There's an enormous loss of life on both sides. He used intelligence practices that are military intelligence gathering techniques. And yet they paid for all this, for the most part, by getting opium and heroin into the U.S. market.[22]

The opium trade begins in the fields when more than a million farmers plant and harvest the annual poppy crop. This segment of the labor force, the largest under the umbrella of a cartel, is the cornerstone of the cartel.

Cultivating Poppies

The opium that will one day end up on the streets of America begins thousands of miles away where Asian farmers cultivate their fields. A household of several members cultivates and harvests about one acre of opium poppy per year on average. Most of the more fertile fields can support cultivation for ten years or more without fertilization before the soil is depleted and new fields must be cleared.

Farmers plant poppy seeds in shallow holes. Within six weeks a cabbagelike plant emerges, and eight weeks later the poppy plant grows to about two feet. At this point, the farmers move through the fields thinning the weaker plants to allow the stronger ones enough room to mature.

Each poppy has one long primary stem and secondary stems called tillers. As the plant grows, one and occasionally two buds develop at the tip. After ninety days, the buds blossom into flowers with four petals in a variety of vibrant colors. When the petals fall away, generally in January, only the green pods remain, and they continue to grow to the size and shape of an egg. Inside the pods the sap of opium develops over ten days while the pods ripen. Once the pods reach maturity, standing on stalks between three and five feet tall, alkaloid production stops. A typical one-acre poppy field has about 100,000 plants that produce 125,000 to 200,000 pods. The actual opium yield will depend largely on weather conditions and the precautions taken by individual farmers to tend and safeguard the crop.

Growing poppies worth thousands of dollars per acre is unlike tending any other crop. The farmer and his family generally move from their homes to the edge of their field two weeks prior to harvest, setting up a small, temporary hut. If they do not, they run the risk of poachers stealing their crop. Ghulam Shan, a poppy

An Afghani opium farmer weeds out the weaker poppy plants in his fields to provide enough room for the stronger plants to thrive.

farmer east of Afghanistan's capital city, Kabul, works for the drug lord Hazrat Ali. Shan tends his fields carrying an AK-47 automatic rifle given to him by Ali to protect his family and his crop.

Harvesting

Harvesting the opium crop requires unusual skill. As the pods reach maturity, harvesters move through the fields in the coolness of the late afternoon selecting only the ripest pods and slitting each with a special, curved knife. The incisions are made with great care to avoid cutting too deeply into the wall of the pod, which causes the opium to drip into the interior of the pod, rather than ooze to the surface where it can be collected. If the incisions are too shallow, the flow is

A Thai harvester uses a flat iron blade to collect the sticky gum from the surface of an opium pod.

too slow and the opium coagulates over the incisions and blocks the flow. To cut perfectly requires considerable practice.

As the milky white sap, or *sheera*, oozes to the surface, it darkens and thickens in the sun, forming a brownish gum called *apeen* or *taryak*. Early the next morning, harvesters scrape the sticky opium gum from the surface of the pods with a short-handled, crescent-shaped, flat iron blade. The opium gum is then scraped into a wood container that hangs from the harvester's neck or waist.

Opium harvesters work their way backward across the field with their elbows tucked tightly to their waists to avoid brushing up against the scored and oozing pods. The pods continue to secrete opium for up to five days until the sap is depleted. During the short harvest period, workers spent each day tending the pods: scoring those newly matured, collecting the sap from previously scored pods, and cutting down and discarding those depleted of their sap.

When harvesters return from their fields after a day of collecting, they scrape the thick sap from their containers, pack it into brick-, pancake-, or ball-shaped forms, and wrap them in a simple material such as banana leaves that will allow the sticky mass to dry. Each harvester then tags his or her bundle with colored string or yarn to keep it separate from those of other harvesters.

Excessive moisture and heat can cause the opium to deteriorate slightly. When an entire field is harvested, owners can expect about ten to fifteen pounds of opium per acre, a number that can fluctuate depending upon environmental variables.

Cooking

Before opium is ready to be sold, it is cooked to remove vegetable matter and other impurities that detract from a high-quality product. To prepare the sap for cooking, farmers and their families chop wood and dig a shallow pit. They dump the opium into a large pot filled with water. The wood is placed in the pit under the pot and set on fire to boil the concoction, causing the sticky glob to dissolve. Any soil, twigs, or plant scrapings remain suspended in their solid form, and when the entire solution is strained, the impurities are captured and discarded.

The filtered brown liquid is then reheated over a low flame until any remaining water evaporates, leaving behind a thick paste called prepared opium, cooked opium, or smoking opium. It is then dried in the sun until it has a putty-like consistency. The net weight of the cooked opium has now dropped by about twenty percent. At this point in the process, most farmers separate 10 or 15 percent of the paste for sale to local users.

The farmers carry the remaining opium to large villages or cities, where buyers examine it, assess its purity, and offer a price. Buyers are skilled at their craft and look for hidden impurities intentionally mixed into the opium to increase its weight and thus its price. Such adulterants include tree sap, sand, flour, and a variety of vegetation ground and colored to camouflage its presence. Once a price is agreed upon, the buyer sells the opium paste to middlemen who own simple factories. There, the paste is further purified, combined into larger quantities, molded into standardized bricks weighing precisely five or ten kilograms (one kilogram equals 2.2 pounds), and wrapped in heavy plastic. The middlemen in turn sell the packaged product at a considerably higher price to a network of international distributors.

Distribution from Asia

Distributors are highly skilled and astute men and women responsible for guiding the opium from rural villages until it reaches its final destinations in London, Moscow, New York, Hong Kong, or any other of a dozen or more metropolitan centers. Shipments of opium travel on the backs of smugglers or goats working their way over jagged mountain passes, on camels across expanses of desert, on dugout canoes paddled down inland rivers, or on trucks to a port where either an oceangoing freighter or a 747 jetliner carries it to its final destination.

Getting opium out of the Golden Crescent or Golden Triangle is a deadly business. In 2003 in Iran, for example, gun battles claimed the lives of 170 Iranian police and more than seven hundred traffickers along a 650-mile antidrug barrier intended to stop smuggling. Reporter Mike Corcoran, who witnessed the smuggling of opium, noted the sophistication of the distribution network:

> The drug runners are armed with the best weapons money can buy—even highly sophisticated Stinger missiles trained on Iran's patrolling helicopters. The head of Iran's Drug Control Headquarters reveals that in one year 200 drug runners were executed for their crimes and another 85,000 are currently serving prison terms on drug related offences.[23]

If distributors elude border guards, they then run a gauntlet of checkpoints once they reach airports and loading docks along wharves. Distributors are masterly at concealing opium in large containers or equipment such as washing machines and truck engines. They also weld packages of opium inside steel construction

Money Laundering

Opium cartels transact business exclusively with cash, preferably U.S. dollars. Any use of checks or credit cards by bosses working outside international law to purchase opium would lead law enforcement to their bank accounts and homes. Yet depositing millions, if not billions, of cash dollars in bank accounts around the world can also attract attention unless opium bosses can show that the cash came from legitimate activities.

The process of changing the identity of cash from drug money to legitimate money is termed money laundering. Once money is laundered, it is impossible for law enforcement to prove where or how it was made and who made it. According to one official who contributed to the "International Narcotics Control Strategy Report," which can be found on the U.S. Department of State Web site, "Money laundering is organized crime's way of trying to disprove the adage that 'crime doesn't pay.' It is an attempt to assure drug dealers that they can hide their profits and to provide them the fuel to operate and expand their criminal enterprises."

One of the most common money-laundering tricks is to take millions of dollars to large gambling casinos such as those found in Las Vegas, Hong Kong, or Paris. Opium bosses purchase gambling chips with opium money, gamble for a few days, and when they are finished, they cash in their remaining chips for casino cash. As they depart with a receipt from the casino, no one can know for certain whether their money came from gambling winnings or not. The actual laundering occurs as the opium cash is exchanged for casino cash. At that point, the identity is lost, or laundered.

An Afghan opium dealer holds thousands of U.S. dollars next to a bag of the narcotic ready for sale.

material, and press them into common, unassuming items such as jewelry boxes, tennis shoes, and food cans emptied of their contents.

The likelihood of passing inspection points trouble free is regularly increased through bribery. Most distributors spend millions of dollars a year bribing inspection officials, from the highest-ranking officers down to the men and women who perform the inspections. The bribes that corrupt inspectors accept can often exceed the amount of their annual salaries. Under such circumstances, no amount of sophisticated monitoring devices, X-ray machines, sensitive odor detectors, or drug-sniffing dogs are able to uncover the contraband.

Once opium shipments reach America, customs officials assisted by the DEA screen as much cargo as possible but openly admit that only a fraction can be searched. The DEA estimates that it is able to intercept about 10 percent of all smuggled drugs, but other agencies charged with interdicting narcotics believe the percentage is more likely half that.

Distribution from Mexico
According to the DEA, the easiest entry for opium smugglers into the United States is across the Mexican border. There are several reasons why this border provides easy access. First, Mexico is an opium-growing nation. Second, it is impossible for law enforcement to patrol the entire border, which stretches all the way from east Texas to California. It is also difficult to monitor the large daily volume of vehicular traffic crossing the border and thousands of Mexicans who illegally move back and forth across it. According to a National Narcotics Intelligence Consumers Committee report, "In recent years, this infrastructure [American opium trafficking] has become heavily dependent on the smuggling services of drug gangs operating from Mexico, which has enabled the drug gangs there to emerge as sophisticated and powerful international drug trafficking organizations within their own right."[24]

Once opium enters America, it is picked up by the next link of the opium alliance, one of many American drug bosses.

The Rise of Mexican Opium

During the 1980s Mexican opium cartels entered the international opium industry by planting their first large opium fields. The geographic climate in much of Mexico is well suited for opium. To an impoverished nation, opium is an attractive crop that can be sold just north of the border in the United States. With long-established trafficking and distribution networks first set up for marijuana and cocaine, Mexico successfully entered into the opium business. Mexico grows only about 3 or 4 percent of the world's opium crop, but virtually all of it is shipped across the border to the United States.

According to a report published by the General Accounting Office in March 1996, *Drug Control—Long-Standing Problems Hinder U.S. International Efforts*, a DEA administrator testified: "Drug trafficking organizations in Mexico have become so wealthy and so powerful over the years transporting opium and cocaine that they can rival legitimate governments for influence and control. They utilize their vast financial wealth to undermine government and commercial institutions. We have witnessed Colombia's struggle with this problem, and it [is] not unexpected that the same problems could very well develop in Mexico."

Just as Asia's production of opium has posed a major threat to America, the DEA anticipates that Mexico's production will increase the tonnage of opium annually smuggled into the United States in cars and trucks passing through dozens of border checkpoints.

American Opium Bosses

American opium bosses control all opium imported into the United States for sale and distribution, operating in a similar manner to opium bosses in Asia and Mexico. According to the Federal Bureau of Investigation (FBI), the majority of American drug bosses belong to one of several crime syndicates that collectively make up the American Mafia.

For more than one hundred years, the Mafia has been actively engaged in a variety of criminal activities, including gambling, drug dealing, prostitution, and extortion. The FBI is constantly monitoring their activities and arresting members whenever sufficient evidence can be gathered to prosecute them.

American bosses rely on bribery and violence to protect their enterprises. Local, state, and federal law enforcement agents

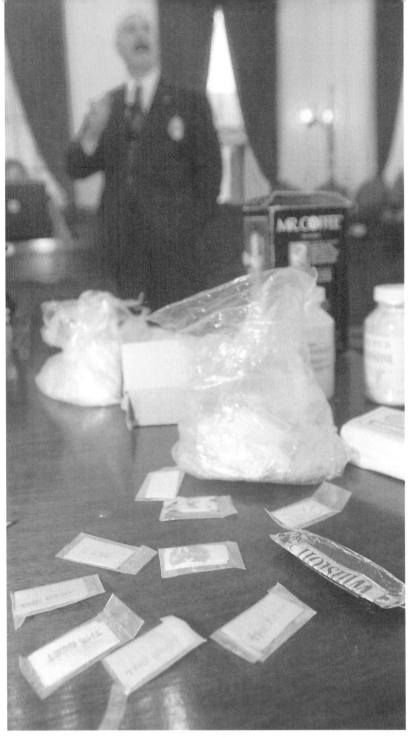

During an antidrug conference, a police captain in Vermont displays bags of heroin to illustrate the problem of addiction in the state.

occasionally accept bribes to conceal illegal opium transactions, although corruption is not nearly as common as in grower nations. Nonetheless, according to Alfred W. McCoy, a Professor of Southeast Asian Studies, bribery finds its way even to high-level American politicians and law enforcement officers:

> American diplomats and secret agents have been involved in the narcotics traffic at three levels: (1) coincidental complicity by allying with groups actively engaged in the drug traffic; (2) abetting the traffic by covering up for known traffickers and condoning their involvement; (3) and active engagement in the transport of opium and heroin. It is ironic, to say the least, that America's opium and heroin plague is of its own making.[25]

Violence is commonly used to control the opium trade. Without access to law enforcement and America's legal system to operate their illegal businesses, crime syndicates provide their own system of justice, which often relies upon violence to force payment of debts and to monopolize the sale of opium in major cities.

High-level members of America's Mafia are tipped off to the cargo locations of the five- and ten-kilogram bricks when they enter the country. Once the bricks are retrieved from their hiding places, the probability that they will be detected drops dramatically because of the impossibility of searching millions of cars, trucks, trains, and buses. Although the top American opium bosses never see, much less touch, the opium, their vast financial resources and their connections with corrupt American officials play a key role in the importation and distribution of the country's opium supply.

The top American bosses usually purchase bulk shipments of bricks totaling twenty-five to one hundred kilos for which they pay several hundred thousand dollars. At this point along the opium route, its value has increased six to seven times the amount the farmers earned in their villages. The average cost for each one-kilogram brick of opium that initially brought peasant farmers $750 is purchased by American bosses from international distributors for about $5,000. After a shipment arrives, the bosses divide it into lots of one to five kilos for sale to their underlings in the organized crime families. A lower-ranking boss, known as a kilo connection, further divides the opium into smaller quantities that are sold to street dealers.

Selling Opium on America's Streets

Street dealers sell opium directly to the final link in the opium alliance, the addicts. Street dealers are often opium addicts who work independently, unaffiliated with any syndicate. They generally purchase opium from a kilo connection in packets known as bundles, which weigh about one ounce and cost roughly two hundred dollars. The street dealers divide the bundles into one-gram quantities called deals or bags. The most commonly distributed amount weighs one gram. Selling for ten dollars, it is known as a

---

Footing the Bill of Corruption

The high profit margins common to the opium business have always been sufficient to bribe authorities to ensure the continuous flow of opium across international borders, from state to state, and from city to city in the United States. At the heart of the bribery scenario—what makes it work so effectively much of the time—is the principle of paying bribes to people in positions of authority that exceed their normal salary.

An example of how money in the form of bribes moves opium occurred in Southeast Asia. A train was used to smuggle opium from Laos to the Vietnamese port city of Da Nang, where a cargo ship would take it to Hawaii. The driver of the train's locomotive, whose monthly railroad salary was $40, was paid an additional $200 for carrying a packet of opium worth $4,000 on each trip. A provincial governor in Laos, however, knowing that smugglers were using the train, promised a railroad inspector the equivalent of his weekly $3 salary for every packet of opium he confiscated. To counter this generous offer, the smugglers paid the same inspector $6 for every undetected packet that found its way to the harbor in Da Nang.

A similar scenario played out onboard the cargo ship, where more inspectors and ship's officers were again paid to look the other way. The opium packet moved across the ocean to Hawaii, where the bribery scheme was again repeated. In all cases, as the opium packet moved around the world, everyone involved was a financial winner. So who foots the bill for all of these illegal transactions? The answer is the last person in this chain of events, the addict.

"dime bag." Occasionally a half-gram amount known as a "nickel bag," is sold for five dollars. Although opium may actually be packaged in bags, the preferred packaging is small party balloons. Balloons are ideal because the dose is easily carried and kept dry. Some addicts, when pursued by police, swallow the balloon to hide the evidence and retrieve it later.

As the nickel and dime bags are distributed and consumed, the opium inflicts its damage. Two of the objectives of America's law enforcement and medical communities are to seize opium before it can be used and to counsel the public to avoid its use before its damage can be done.

Chapter 4

The Costs of America's Opium Problem

A merica faces a pandemic of drug abuse that inflicts staggering costs on the nation. The United States constitutes just one segment of the global illicit drug market, yet according to the UNDCP, its population consumes a disproportionately large percentage of the world's estimated eight-thousand-ton opium crop.

The profile of America's opium problem takes many shapes. On the one hand, the profile includes those addicted to the drug and those who supply the addicts by smuggling, distributing, and selling the contraband. To the people involved in activities that violate the law, the costs can be devastating. Many spend much of their lives in jail, while addicts who manage to avoid arrest and sentencing pay a moral cost by neglecting themselves, their families, and their jobs in a never-ending quest to purchase their next fix. On the other hand, the profile includes legions of federal, state, and local law enforcement agencies, branches of the military, the medical community, and private citizen groups trying to stamp out opium. The costs of the opium industry to these groups and to all Americans is an estimated annual $8 billion to detect, seize, prosecute, incarcerate, and treat thousands of opium smugglers, distributors, and addicts.

Twentieth-Century Moral Condemnation

By 1900 there were an estimated four hundred thousand addicts and an additional six hundred thousand casual opium users in America. Within churches, community town halls, and the halls of Congress, a moral aversion to the expansion of opium abuse and its costs to communities had inspired a prohibition movement. For the first time ever, a movement was succeeding in pressuring Congress to enact laws that restricted what Americans could or could not put into their bodies.

In 1912, Dr. John Witherspoon, later president of the American Medical Association, noted the moral costs of opium use in terms of ruined lives and destroyed families and exhorted the medical community to eliminate the opium supply: "Save our people from the clutches of this hydra-headed monster which stalks abroad through the civilized world, wrecking lives and happy homes, filling our jails and lunatic asylums [mental hospitals], and taking from these unfortunates, the precious promise of eternal life."[26]

In 1914 Congress passed the Harrison Act, which placed opium under federal restriction and outlawed the sale, possession, and use of opium. Legitimate opium use by the medical profession ceased with the advent of gas mixtures used as anesthetics and more sophisticated analgesics that are less addictive than opium. Therefore, all opium now brought into America is smuggled to either begin or support addiction.

When Congress outlawed the possession of opium, organized crime syndicates stepped in to provide an uninterrupted flow of opium to users and in so doing created a new multibillion-dollar industry. To enforce the new opium laws and counter organized crime, a variety of law enforcement agencies worked to suppress the crime syndicates.

The crusade of law enforcement to eliminate organized opium dealers and confiscate their contraband stiffened in the late 1950s. In 1996 Martin Booth reported in his book *Opium: A History*, "It has been reckoned that 50 percent of all crime committed in American cities are drug related: this figure may be considerably

In this illustration from 1899, police raid an opium den in New York's Chinatown.

higher in inner-city zones."[27] Although crime committed by opium addicts, dealers, and smugglers represents only about 15 percent of all drug-related crime, law enforcement agencies continue to join in the struggle to remove opium from the nation's streets.

Casual Opium Use

Clearly, high moral and financial costs are attributed to opium abuse and addiction in America. Addiction begins with casual opium use. Opium may be enjoyed once in a while as an intoxicant in metropolitan areas as well as in camps of migratory workers living in tents scattered throughout hundreds of America's agricultural areas. Initially, those who take low opium doses, especially when it is eaten rather than smoked or injected, may not become addicted until they have been taking the drug for months or even years. In some cases, casual users are able to control their intake and never become addicts. For other users, this is not true.

Users such as this Russian heroin addict help fuel the international opium trade.

Some casual users depend upon opium's analgesic effects in place of proper medical attention. Among middle- and low-income families where earnings are insufficient to afford proper health care, opium is used as a means of self-medication. Temporary periods of intense pain from work-related injuries, migraine headaches, and back injuries are self-medicated with small doses of opium. For many workers, particularly those working as field hands, bending over all day picking low-lying fruits and vegetables, back pain becomes a chronic problem they treat with occasional low doses of opium.

Other casual users admit using opium for temporary psychological relief of common anxiety, sleeplessness, loneliness, and sadness. To soften the impact of short-term emotional distress, opium is used as a substitute for psychiatric counseling sessions that can cost between $100 and $150 per hour and can continue weekly for several months to a year. The most common reasons cited for opium use are to relieve depression following the death of a close family member, divorce, and job loss. Regardless of the reasons people begin to use opium, the pleasurable feelings the drug provides prompt them to continue or increase use.

Casual opium use can occur without impairing the user's health. When small amounts are taken occasionally, the body recovers and repairs any damage to the cardiovascular system. The same claims cannot be made, however, when high doses are taken regularly.

America's Opium Addicts

Most opium addicts in the United States hide their addiction, rarely speaking publicly about it. One of America's most well-known poets of the mid–twentieth century, Williams Burroughs, was a confessed opium addict willing to speak openly about his addiction on behalf of those who could not. In an interview in 1956, he discussed his problem, with startling honesty about his use and attitude toward addiction:

> Over a period of twelve years I have used opium, smoked and taken orally, injected in skin, vein, muscle, and sniffed when no needle was available. In

all cases, the end result will be the same: addiction. And a smoking habit is as difficult to break as an intravenous injection habit. The use of opium leads to a metabolic dependence on opium. Opium becomes a biologic need just as water.[28]

Statistics indicate that the pool of American opium addicts is older than for any other type of drug addiction; about 45 percent are over forty, 45 percent are between twenty-five and forty, and 10 percent are younger than twenty-five. One explanation for this phenomenon was the dramatic increase of opium use and addiction following the end of the Vietnam War in the mid-1970s, when returning troops brought opium and opium addiction home with them. DEA statistics further indicate that 83 percent of addicts are male.

Pictured at work, American poet William S. Burroughs spoke candidly of his opium addiction.

The National Institute of Mental Health (NIMH) divides opium addicts into two general camps, those capable of controlling their addiction well enough to find employment and those who cannot. The NIMH estimates that about 65 percent of opium addicts are capable of maintaining some sort of employment. The problem, however, is that employment is rarely long-term and rarely pays well. Most addicts do not qualify for high-paying jobs because they focus more on their next fix than on their work. Some addicts can control their needs to complete an eight-hour shift, but the last hour or two brings on depression and irritation with coworkers and management.

Interview with an Opium Smoker

A San Francisco woman was arrested for opium possession. Her interview with arresting officers about her addiction can be found in *The Consumers Union Report on Licit and Illicit Drugs*, on the Drug Library Web site.

Q. Why did you start to smoke opium?

A. Why do people start to drink? Trouble, I suppose, led me to smoke. I think it is better than drinking. People who smoke opium do not kick up rows; they injure no one but themselves, and I do not think they injure themselves very much.

Q. Why do you smoke now?

A. Because I must; I could not live without it. I smoke partly because of the quiet enjoyment it gives, but mainly to escape from the horrors which would ensue if I did not smoke. To go twenty-four hours without smoking is to suffer worse tortures than can be believed.

Q. Then why do you return to the use of the drug?

A. Ah! that's it; there is a time when my hands fail me; tears fall from my eyes, I am ready to sink; then I come here and have a smoke, which sets me right. There is too much nonsense talked about opium-smoking. Life without it would be unendurable. I am in excellent health; but, I suppose, every one has their own troubles, and I have mine.

Q. Are women of your class [blue collar] generally addicted to opium-smoking?

A. No; they are more addicted to alcohol, and alcohol does them far more harm. When a woman drinks she gets into more trouble pretty quick.

The other 35 percent are incapable of any sort of normal social interactions, let alone employment. This group tends to survive on some sort of criminal activity to support their addiction as well as to acquire food, clothing, and shelter. Most addicts live in large American cities, because there they can congregate and work as pushers who sell opium to addicts as well as recruit new addicts. Often, living in apartments shared by several opium users or pushers, many addicts run afoul of the law by supplementing their income with armed robbery, street muggings, and auto theft.

Neglected Lives of Opium Addicts

Many new opium users quit after a few months on the drug's roller-coaster ride of euphoria and depression, yet others continue to use it for many years or become repeat customers for life. Eventually, many addicts are arrested, sentenced, and sometimes sent to jail. One such man who experienced this, a San Franciscan who asked for anonymity, had this to say about his opium use and eventual incarceration:

> Five years ago I was editor and manager of a metropolitan newspaper. Today I am a convict serving my second penitentiary sentence. Between these extremes is a single cause—opium. For five years I have been a smoker of opium. For five years there has not been a day, scarcely an hour, during which my mind and body have not been under the influence of the most subtle and insidious of drugs. And now, after weeks of agony in a prison, I am myself again, a normal-minded man, able to look back critically and impartially over the ruinous past. If I can set down here fairly and simply the story of those years, I will have done something that may save many others.[29]

In addition to leading lives of crime and poverty, many addicts suffer severe medical problems relating to excessive opium use, which takes its toll on the body. Long-term opium use is destructive to the health of the addict. Users with medical complications often show up in emergency rooms: Cardiac arrest, stroke, and liver failure are all well-documented results of excessive opium use. In addition to these traumas to the body, the addict's appetite also suffers. Continuous use of opium reduces a person's appetite, leading to a variety of illnesses due to malnutrition. According to

Long-term addicts like this heroin user in Poland are at high risk for developing a host of serious medical conditions.

Jonathan Spence of Yale University, those who manage to maintain a healthy appetite suffer less than those who do not: "Those who eat regularly and well do not suffer physiologically from their addiction, but for the poor, addiction is a serious health hazard, since shortages of cash resources are put to opium rather than food purchases."[30]

Additional health hazards affect those who smoke opium. The heat of burning opium and a variety of carcinogens inhaled with the opium pose the potential for lung damage and in severe cases lung cancer. When opium burns, it releases dozens of hot gases that damage the lung tissue, and even the cooled-down gases carried by the blood adversely affect heart valves and blood pressure. Biopsies of lung tissue taken from long-term addicts reveal that the minute and delicate alveoli cells of the lungs are badly scarred.

Numerous conditions are linked to the other ways in which opium is consumed. Some of these illnesses are commonly found among those who take opium intravenously, a practice known as shooting or mainlining. Injecting drugs often leads to the damage or collapse of veins. Addicts who shoot opium also have the problem of finding clean needles because they are illegal without a doctor's prescription. Consequently, users often share needles with others without first properly cleaning them. Sharing dirty needles places users at high risk of contracting human immunodeficiency virus (HIV) and deadly infectious diseases such as hepatitis. Nobody knows how many addicts contract HIV and hepatitis in this manner, but according to the National Institute on Drug Abuse, shooting illicit drugs, including opium, is the leading risk factor for new cases of infectious diseases.

The problem with opium addicts became so severe in the 1950s that medical practitioners coordinated their efforts to help addicts by providing a variety of psychological therapies they hoped would cure addiction.

Opium Addiction Therapy

Nineteenth-century opium users and physicians recognized the powerfully addictive nature of opium, but it was not until the mid–twentieth century that therapeutic strategies were implemented to release addicts from its grip. Since the 1950s, three therapies have been recognized as providing some limited value for addicts: psychological, sociological, and biochemical.

A variety of psychological therapies were tried first. At the heart of all of them was the belief that addiction resided in the psyche or personality of the addict. There were many variations on this theme, including the belief that addicts acquired a predisposition toward addiction in early childhood caused by such problems as poor parental judgment, acute poverty, and domestic violence. To proponents of this theory, recovery might be found during therapy sessions, occurring as often as three times a week over a three- to four-year period, in which the addict revisited his or her childhood by remembering and sharing painful events with a therapist. In theory, the healing process occurred while discussing the painful memories with the doctor. A variation of this therapy described addiction as the result of conflicts in the addict's adult life resulting from traumatic events such as divorce, job loss, or death of a family member. Whether the therapy focused on childhood or adult traumas, the goal was a restructuring of the personality to cope with life without opium.

During the 1980s, a variety of sociologically based therapies expressed the view that societal circumstances caused addiction. Doctors subscribing to sociologically based therapies believed that factors leading to addiction could include the hopelessness of living in inner-city slums, a lack of optimism brought on by poverty, boredom triggered by low income or meaningless, repetitive jobs, and a general sense of malaise, especially in those associated with teenage street gangs. Therapists who accepted the sociological model treated opium addicts in group therapy sessions of five to twenty addicts. During group sessions, the therapist forced each addict to honestly confront and discuss the reasons for abusing opium and to identify factors that triggered the need for a fix. Once the triggering factors were identified, the healing process occurred by avoiding them. Common triggering factors included friendships with other addicts, boredom brought on by cutting school or failing to go to work, and gang membership. In all cases, the common theme was the belief that addiction could be cured by engaging in healthier social contacts.

The most recent theory of opium addiction is the biochemical theory, which says that addiction is caused by chemical reactions in the brain. In this theory, the acute withdrawal symptoms suffered after an addict is deprived of opium are biochemical in origin. The cause of these immediate withdrawal symptoms is in the structure of the chemical molecule and its effect on cells of the nervous system. Exposed regularly to opium molecules, the human nervous system adjusts to its presence and in so doing becomes dependent upon it. When the opium molecules are withdrawn, the nervous system becomes seriously affected.

Biochemical therapy involves the use of chemicals to block the cravings without adversely affecting the addict. The most commonly used chemical is methadone, a synthetic drug taken orally once a day that is capable of suppressing opium withdrawal symptoms.

Methadone

For more than thirty years the synthetic narcotic methadone has been used to treat opium addiction. Research and clinical studies show that long-term methadone treatment, taken under medical supervision, has no adverse effect on the heart, lungs, liver, kidneys, bones, blood, brain, or other vital body organs, and it produces no serious side effects.

In addition, methadone does not impair cognitive functions. It has no adverse effects on mental capability, intelligence, or employability. It is not sedating or intoxicating like opium, and it does not interfere with ordinary activities such as driving a car or operating machinery. Patients are able to feel pain and experience emotional reactions. Most important, methadone relieves the craving associated with opium addiction.

Under a physician's supervision, methadone is administered orally on a daily basis at a cost of thirteen dollars per dose. Because its effects will last all day, the cost is considerably lower than what an opium addict would spend for multiple doses. Because the dose is taken orally, addicts do not run the risk of contracting or spreading HIV/AIDS or hepatitis through the use of dirty needles.

Methadone is not a panacea, however. Many people argue that substituting one drug for another does not solve the addicts' real problems. Some ultimately remain addicted to methadone, requiring continuous treatment, sometimes over a period of years.

A patient takes a daily dose of methadone to treat his opium addiction.

Methadone reduces the cravings associated with opium use, but it does not provide any pleasurable experiences. Consequently, methadone patients do not experience the extreme highs and lows that result from the waxing and waning of opium. This theory is controversial in that ultimately, the patient remains physically dependent on methadone.

Most Americans agree that opium addicts who seek help should get it. A debate, however, centers on determining the best strategy for curing the addict. This debate prompted the General Accounting Office (GAO) of the federal government to investigate the effectiveness of various drug therapies. In 1996 the GAO published the results of a lengthy study focused on opium and other addictive drugs. The study concluded that no one was certain how much success any of the therapies had provided:

America's Army of Opium Chasers

The United States has an army of governmental agencies hot on the trail of opium and opium dealers before they reach America's shores. To aggressively confront opium distribution, many federal law enforcement agencies swing into action to suppress opium before it arrives.

The first of America's lines of defense is the military, especially the Coast Guard. American warships regularly cruise international waters in search of ships that may be transporting opium and other illicit drugs. When ships suspected of carrying drugs are spotted, American warships force them to stop while sailors with opium-sniffing dogs board them and prowl the corridors, engine rooms, and cargo holds. If opium is uncovered, the ship is escorted to the nearest U.S. port and is impounded until the conclusion of legal action.

Assisting the military is the Drug Enforcement Administration another arm of the federal government. Founded in 1973, DEA is charged with coordinating all drug enforcement and confiscation activities in the United States well as foreign countries. The DEA coordinates its efforts with foreign governments, usually those of poppy-growing nations, to curtail the growth and harvest of the drug.

A third arm that assists in controlling the flow of opium is the Federal Bureau of Investigation. It inspect companies suspected of trafficking in illegal drugs and foods arrests and prosecutes anyone caught distributing large quantities of opium.

Although studies conducted over three decades consistently show that treatment reduces drug use and crime, current data collection techniques do not allow accurate measurement of the extent to which treatment reduces the use of illicit drugs. Furthermore, research literature has not yet yielded definitive evidence to identify which approaches work best for specific groups of drug abusers.[31]

The conclusion of the GAO report that the best therapeutic approaches have not yet been identified piqued the interest of many specialists working in the field of drug rehabilitation. After much research, therapists have concluded that no single therapy can be identified as being the best for all addicts and that the best strategy is for the addict and his or her therapist to explore several. Experts have also concluded that whichever therapies are applied, the addict must understand that there are no short-term solutions to the complexities of opium addiction.

The Role of American Law Enforcement

While doctors struggle to assist addicts to free themselves from their agony, law enforcement officers grapple with the task of confiscating opium before it can reach more users. Suppression of the opium trade has been one of American law enforcement's objectives since 1914, when Congress outlawed opium's general use. Today all law enforcement agencies—federal, state, and local—coordinate their efforts to discourage the use of opium with a three-pronged strategy of border seizures, arrests and prosecutions of those smuggling and selling opium, and incarceration of those convicted. The implementation of these strategies is enormously expensive. Trying to calculate the financial costs is impossible, because dozens of independent law enforcement agencies, multiple layers of the court system, attorneys, the penitentiary system, and the military commit resources to suppress opium. Nonetheless, the dollar amount is in the tens of billions annually.

The U.S. border is the primary line of defense for seizing opium. Customs officers are authorized to inspect any person, vehicle, container, or object that they suspect may conceal contraband. News reports often dramatically chronicle the arrests of smugglers and seizures of opium. Customs officials and border

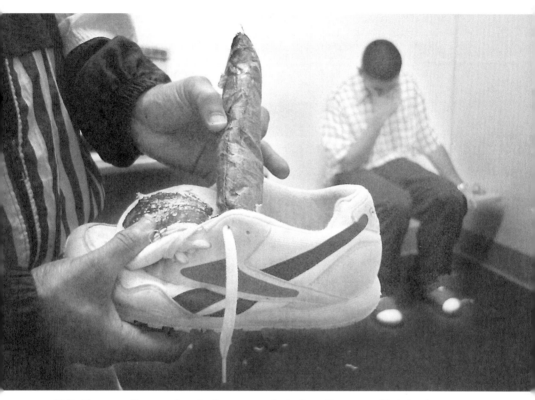

U.S. Customs discovers heroin in a smuggler's shoe. Customs officials often seize heroin and other opiates at border crossings across the United States.

patrol officers cite these seizures as evidence of America's success in the war on drugs.

Using aircraft to counter the smuggling threat, the DEA equips planes with infrared cameras and radar to detect, track, and intercept smugglers' aircraft. Military aircraft bristling with sophisticated detection devices make flights from Florida and Texas deep into Central America's airspace to search for questionable aircraft flying north. When suspicious aircraft are spotted, their positions are radioed to intercept aircraft, which follow the suspect planes to their destinations, where they are searched.

The task of interdiction within the United States is a daunting one. Once opium is inside the United States, preventing its distribution and use is difficult. As large bulk shipments are broken into small packets, they are easily concealed for distribution anywhere in the United States. Law enforcement relies upon tips from paid informers, arrested opium addicts, and sophisticated surveillance to seize street-level quantities and arrest the dealers. Agencies such as the DEA are experimenting with new tactics as well. The Mobile Enforcement Team program responds to the drug-related violent crime that plagues certain urban neighborhoods, while Operations Pipeline and Convoy target motor vehicles, stopping and inspecting suspicious vehicles on the nation's highways.

Despite the best efforts of the DEA and other government agencies at intercepting the supply and punishing traffickers with jail time, the amount of opium available on America's streets remains large. The opium problem is the result of American addicts who want the drugs and foreign suppliers who profit handsomely by growing poppies and selling opium. These two forces combine to make opium a tricky international political problem.

Chapter 5

The International Politics of Opium

Moving forward into the twenty-first century, the battle against the international opium trade presents a complex political, social, economic, and cultural dilemma. The world has become a global battleground pitting poppy-growing nations that financially profit from the drug against opium-consuming nations that lose financially and morally. Two leading American anthropologists, Sidney Mintz and Eric Wolf, have written extensively about opium's economic impact on global politics, emphasizing that opium is one commodity that has "shaped the politics, culture, and social structure of peoples around the globe. . . . Opium is a key commodity in the expanding commerce between Asia and the Atlantic nations, thereby becoming enmeshed in the politics, economies, and cultures of both regions."[32]

As thousands of tons of opium move annually across international trade routes, leaders of all involved nations apportion blame for the scourge. Government and civic leaders in the consumer nations blame the growing nations for allowing poppies to be harvested, while the growing nations blame consumer nations for allowing drug use and addiction within their own population.

The conflict simmers among politicians, the lines of the battle are drawn, with national interests of one group at odds with the national interests of the other. Every suggestion for curtailing the international flow of opium is invariably favorable to one side or the other, but rarely both.

Growing Nations Versus Consuming Nations

The distinction between growing and consuming nations is principally economic. The monetary profile of growing nations is one of poverty in which people are dependent upon simple agricultural activities still driven by slow and often inefficient human and animal labor. According to Angelika Schuckler, a farm management economist for the United Nations Food and Agriculture Organization (UNFAO), "You have to tackle the root causes of why farmers grow poppies. We have identified a number of root causes, the main ones being poverty, indebtedness, unemployment, and lack of governance."[33]

Poverty is a key factor that drives people like this woman in Colombia into opium production.

Consuming nations, on the other hand, are wealthy and enjoy highly diversified economies that are based on industry and make use of the latest technologies. To the citizens of consuming nations, the faraway poppy fields represent the source and cause of agony for tens of thousands of homeless, unemployed addicts who loiter on urban streets. Opium addicts face a major health threat and pose an unnecessary economic drain and a socially destructive crime problem. From the point of view of consumer nations, the solution to addiction is to stop the opium trade at its roots, in the nations where the plant grows.

The farmers of poppy-growing nations, however, view the situation very differently. Poppy fields represent a guaranteed income for a large segment of rural populations, and poppies are the most lucrative crop they can grow. Small peasant farmers, whether in Afghanistan, Laos, or Mexico, can easily earn between ten and twenty times more money per acre for poppies than for bananas, coffee, sugar, or wheat.

Opium has been a lifesaver for Ghulam Shah, a thirty-five-year-old Afghan farmer who could barely feed his family on the few hundred dollars a year he earned growing wheat. But in 2002, Shah produced enough opium to pay all his debts and take his teenage daughter to Pakistan for kidney surgery. He estimates his 2003 opium crop will be worth roughly nine thousand dollars, a fortune in a country where most people earn less than one dollar a day. Pleased to be growing poppies, Shah confided in an interview, "Now I can fill my family's stomachs, send my daughter to school, and sleep well."[34] Colonel Pairat Thongjatu, a spokesman for Thailand's army, makes the same observation: "Because a half-acre plot of opium poppies could generate income of up to $9,090 per crop, many poor farmers continue to cultivate poppies despite the legal risks."[35]

At the core of the dilemma is the reality that the poppies that provide an escape from poverty for millions of peasant farmers contribute to the poverty and misery of millions of users. These users include those who abuse opium, morphine, and heroin, since all three drugs are derived from poppies. In an attempt to help

both growers and users, user nations proposed a strategy to eliminate poppy fields while providing either financial compensation or
a viable alternative crop that would prevent farmers from falling
back into poverty. The first strategy suggested and paid for by user
nations was an eradication program aimed at destroying the poppies in the fields.

Poppy Eradication

DEA officers working with British drug enforcement agents sur-
mised that the easiest place to stop the production of opium
might be in the fields, the only place along the international
drug route where the contraband cannot be hidden in containers, moved clandestinely in the night, or compressed into a small,
highly concentrated form difficult to detect. One DEA official
stated the solution this way:

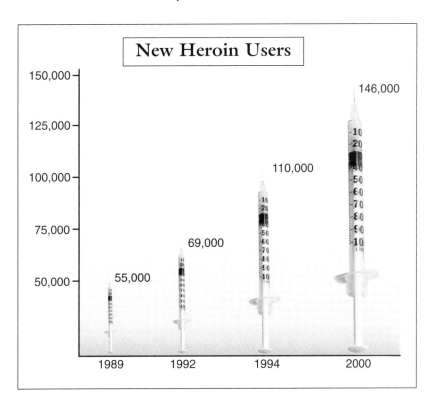

The closer to the source we can attack, the better our chances of halting drug flows altogether. Crop control is by far the most cost-effective means of cutting supply. When crops are destroyed, no drugs can enter the system. It is akin to removing a malignant tumor before it can metastasize [spread]. In a perfect world, with no drug crops to harvest, no drugs could enter the distribution chain. Nor would there be any need for costly enforcement and interdiction operations.[36]

The U.S. and British governments approached several poppy-growing countries with the offer to pay for eradication. Although the logic seemed unassailable, the implementation was not. The

In April 2004 Afghan officials destroy opium poppies as part of an eradication program.

millions of Asian and South American farmers who derive their livelihood from poppies feared that the eradication program would throw them back into poverty. As an incentive, the United States offered each farmer a stipend of between six hundred dollars and eight hundred dollars for each acre destroyed, and Great Britain offered three times that amount. Yet farmers resisted the offers because they knew that a good acre of opium poppies would pay even more. Despite the farmers' protests, many governments agreed to the deal.

Two eradication techniques were tried. The first was to hire local law enforcement officials to travel to known poppy fields, pay the farmer the agreed-upon eradication stipend, and destroy the plants. Swinging long leather whips weighted on the tail end by a small lead ball, police moved through the fields breaking the stalks and laying down the crop.

In larger, more open areas, helicopters equipped with spraying gear were deployed. Loaded with several hundred gallons of herbicides, they swooped low over the fields to spray the toxins. Within minutes of contact, the entire plant shriveled and died. Helicopters were effective and popular with the governments paying the costs. This method of eradication was unpopular, however, with farmers living near the exfoliated fields, who were not compensated for the bordering edible crops the herbicide had destroyed. Unusual skin rashes, burning eyes, an increase in miscarriages, and an assortment of other medical problems among farmers were blamed on the drifting herbicide carried by the winds.

Complaints also came from nonfarmers. Some village mayors objected to what they perceived as harsh military tactics used by law enforcement officers and helicopter crews, who often swept through fields without notice. Even more complaints were lodged by villagers whose income came from cleaning the harvested opium sap, processing, and distributing it. They were not compensated.

What appeared to be a success for consumer nations was not. Although a considerable number of acres were destroyed, the volume of opium, morphine, and heroin sold on the streets barely decreased. The policy of poppy eradication was harshly criticized within growing nations as being a health hazard and an economic flop. To counter these complaints, a second program was proposed that would provide alternative crops to opium farmers.

Alternatives to Poppy Cultivation

The climate in which poppies thrive is suitable for many food crops. The U.S. government, in concert with several other governments, offered poppy farmers alternative crops such as wheat, coffee, bananas, citrus fruits, and a variety of vegetables. The incentive came in the form of better crop seeds, improved farming techniques, and irrigation systems, all at no cost to the farmers. In addition to agricultural assistance, the United States paid farmers in some areas a onetime subsidy for every acre of poppies replaced by food crops.

In Myanmar, a project named Project Hell-Flower was designed to encourage the exchange of opium seeds for a variety of seeds for edible crops. According to Myanmar government spokesman Colonel Hla Min, "We have been implementing ways and means to bring these farmers out of poppy cultivation in a more humanitarian way than resorting to sending in troops to destroy their sole livelihood."[37]

In Pakistan opium farmers in rugged and largely inaccessible foothills will soon be shifting from illicit poppy cultivation to growing legal crops. An estimated thirty thousand tribal people are expected to give up poppy farming and take up the cultivation of alternative crops under a federal government project. Most alternative crops were food crops, flavoring for food such as vanilla, and crops like patchouli that are used in perfumes. J.P. Choudhury, a district magistrate in Pakistan, said, "The project has been given a final shape. The whole idea is to woo the opium farmers into taking up cultivation of high return crops like vanilla and patchouli instead of poppy."[38]

In February 2004, the UNFAO appealed for cash from the United Nations to encourage farmers in Afghanistan to grow crops other than opium. The organization wants donors to provide $25.5 million to finance a number of agricultural development projects be-

Why Is Afghanistan the World's Leading Opium Producer?

Afghanistan is the source of the majority of the opium sold in the world, even though the United States and Great Britain have spent tens of millions of dollars trying to stamp out the country's war-torn but resurgent drug production business. The UN Drug Control Program estimates that between 115,000 and 165,000 acres of land in Afghanistan is dedicated to opium poppy cultivation. Many people involved in suppressing the opium trade have asked how one country could possibly be responsible for growing between 75 and 80 percent of the world's opium supply.

The two principal reasons are related to Afghanistan's geography. First is the remote nature of most of Afghanistan's countryside. Poppies cover fields and hillsides many miles from small villages served by nothing more than narrow dirt roads. These remote areas are rarely visited by government officials, and those who do occasionally arrive do so in cars and trucks unsuited for the desolate, rugged terrain. Lacking gas stations, road signs, and reliable maps, the villages are safe from the prying eyes of outsiders.

The second reason for Afghanistan's proliferation of opium is its location, immediately south of three new nations formed after the collapse of the Soviet Union in 1989. Afghanistan's opium flows north uninterrupted on its way to Europe and the United States because these three nations—Tajikistan, Uzbekistan, and Turkmenistan—have new governments that are under pressure to improve their struggling economies and resolve long-standing internal tribal disputes. Because of their political and economic stresses, the governments of the three northern neighbors pay little attention to Afghanistan's opium trade.

tween 2004 and 2009 in the hope they will wean Afghanistan farmers from the lucrative production of poppies. UNFAO spokeswoman Angelika Schuckler commented, "Rural poverty and a shortage of revenue are the main reasons why farmers produce opium. What is needed is a long-term commitment, probably for more than 10 years to create opportunities for alternative sources of income."[39]

Crop replacement, however, has had only limited success. Its most obvious shortcoming is that alternate crops do not pay as well as opium. In the years 2002 and 2003, the average price for cultivating an acre of food crops in Afghanistan, for example, was only $360, significantly below what opium could bring. In 2004, the president of Afghanistan, Hamid Karzai, commented, "Alternate crops have left many farmers with no choice but to produce narcotics."[40]

The farmers' motives for selling opium poppies occasionally extends beyond simply providing incomes for their families. Because farmers have become relatively wealthy from growing opium, some are willing to spend their opium profits to gain political and social justice from oppressive governments.

Narco-Revolutionaries

As a valued commodity worldwide, opium generates huge profits that can be used to finance a variety of ventures that have the potential to change the way populations live. Beginning in the 1980s, political, social, and economic forces within several poppy-growing nations converged, giving opium the power to topple governments.

Within Colombia, Myanmar, and regions of Afghanistan, Mexico, Pakistan, and Indonesia, bloody civil insurrections are now being fought to overthrow either national or local governments. In all cases, rebel groups claim their aim is to secure greater political and economic freedom for their impoverished rural followers.

Waging a guerrilla war is an expensive proposition for peasant rebels. In opium-producing nations the only source of ready money—enough to purchase automatic weapons, hand grenades, and land mines—is the local opium crop. To gain an equal footing against government forces, rebel forces regularly commandeer and sell some portion of the opium crop and then purchase weapons with the proceeds for their wars of independence.

Since the only big source of money is tied to opium, rebel leaders have tightened their control of the poppy harvests. In some areas, rebel leaders have taken control of the entire industry, from planting and harvesting to packaging and exportation. A portion of the profit is then distributed to the farmers and a portion is used to purchase arms. In regions where this has occurred, government forces have adopted the tactic of destroying poppy fields to limit purchases of weapons. Yet as government troops destroy peasant poppy fields, the major source of income for farmers, the peasants' animosity toward the government is strengthened.

In the regions where rebel activities are most intense, the relationship between the opium crop and the guerrilla warfare is blurred to the point where one cannot exist without the other. In such places, government leaders have pejoratively labeled the revolutionaries "narco-revolutionaries" or "narco-terrorists" because rebels depend on the opium harvests to wage war and because rebel leaders have pressured local farmers to increase rather than decrease poppy production.

Insurrectionists rely on the illicit harvest of opium to attain their political and social objectives. Legitimate governments also involve themselves with opium in crafting their domestic and

An antinarcotics police unit in Colombia raids an opium farm controlled by guerrilla rebels.

Opium as a Tourist Industry

A few regions in the Golden Crescent and the Golden Triangle have attempted to give up growing opium poppies in exchange for tourist dollars. Following the deaths of hundreds of villagers due to local drug wars, chieftains decided to attract tourist dollars to bolster local economies.

Deep within the infamous Golden Triangle along the Thailand-Myanmar border, Western tourists now see an endless stream of camera and film shops, food stalls, hotels topped with satellite dishes, and curio shops selling Golden Triangle T-shirts with photographs of blooming opium fields. A handful of villages that were once havens for opium producers, smugglers, and addicts have learned that tourists fascinated with the opium business will spend money to visit the area.

High on the list for tourists are souvenir opium pipes and other paraphernalia associated with smoking opium, such as small leather bags and tiny ceramic pots traditionally used to carry small amounts of opium and tiny oil lamps used to light the opium. Also of interest to visitors are opium dens that tour guides claim are authentic. As tourists are led inside, they witness what they are told are opium addicts reclining on wooden beds in a semiconscious state. Along the perimeter of the room, pipes, opium lamps, and satchels used to store the opium lend an authentic look.

Local entrepreneurs eager to cash in on the exotic mystique of the opium trade provide adventure cruises along small rivers where guides narrate the dangers of smuggling opium. As the boatmen paddle the canoes, a guide points to landing sites where they claim the drug is clandestinely sold. Further downstream they pass other small boats that the guides allege are used to transport opium. Whether the stories are true or merely invention, tourists enjoy what appears to be a thrilling and dangerous tour.

foreign policies. One such case involving a consumer nation and a grower nation is the current relationship between the United States and Afghanistan. Fields of opium poppies play a central role in the relationship between the two countries and their political objectives.

Politicians' Interest in Opium

Fields flooded with blooming opium poppies attract the attention of more than just farmers and opium bosses; legitimate politicians keep an eye on them as well. Any venture involving billions of dollars and providing the livelihood for millions of people is of interest to politicians, and the illegal opium trade is no exception. Although most governments publicly denounce the opium industry, they also know that opium production must be approached diplomatically. They understand that allowing the growth of poppies is often in their interests and those of their nations.

Within poppy-growing countries, politicians often turn a blind eye to poppy fields in exchange for political support. For example, a 2003 United Nations survey, revealed that the income of all Afghanistan poppy farmers was equivalent to half of all legitimate businesses in that country. Of greater concern to the authors of the survey, however, was the level of involvement of high-ranking officials that makes poppy eradication difficult if not impossible. As the authors claim, "Out of this drug chest, some government administrators and military commanders take a considerable share: the more they get used to this, the less likely it becomes that they will respect the law, be loyal to Kabul [Afghanistan's capital], and support the legal economy."[41]

When many influential Afghans profit from the opium trade, few politicians are willing to get rid of it. President Hamid Karzai denounces the crop but cannot afford to alienate his supporters, many of whom are poppy farmers and drug bosses. Two journalists, Alexander Cockburn and Jeffrey St. Clair, stated, "In political terms, it's a safe forecast to say that no serious effort will be made to interfere with the opium crop. To do so would be to deal the Karzai regime a serious blow."[42]

America's Foreign Policy

Karzai's refusal to attack the opium harvest has implications for the United States. In 2001, American military forces invaded Afghanistan to avenge the September 11, 2001, attacks on the World Trade Center and the Pentagon. Their objective was to eliminate the man who took responsibility for the attacks, Osama bin Laden, and the Taliban government that supported him. After chasing the Taliban and bin Laden throughout Afghanistan, the

United States chose Karzai to rule the country. In exchange for generous sums of money and military support, the United States made three requests of Karzai: establish a democracy, eradicate the last elements of the Taliban, and destroy the poppy fields.

Foreign policy analysts have praised Karzai for solid progress toward the first two objectives but not the third. Karzai has refused to act aggressively against the opium trade because of its lucrative income to those whose support is essential to Karzai's government. Although U.S. officials decry his reluctance to suppress the poppy crop, they are willing to tolerate it because, as one American official said, "Any intense eradication effort could imperil the stability of the government and hamper America's military campaign against the Taliban."[43]

Reports have surfaced that President George W. Bush's administration has given up hope of reducing Afghanistan's opium trade. According to a 2002 article in the *New York Times*, "The U.S. government has 'quietly abandoned' efforts to reduce the crop this year. Instead, the U.S. will resort to a policy of persuading Afghan leaders to carry out a modest eradication program, if only

To maintain the support of Afghan drug bosses, President Hamid Karzai does little to prevent opium farmers like this one from growing their crop.

The One Success

In 2000, according to the UN Drug Control Program, the poppy harvest in Afghanistan produced 3,276 tons of raw opium. This volume had roughly stayed the same for several years, and at the time there was no reason to assume it would dramatically change. But in 2001 it did, dropping to just 185 tons, the lowest levels ever recorded by the UNDCP.

This 94 percent decline in opium production was startling news to the world's law enforcement agencies, which had never been able to achieve much more than a 5 percent reduction in the drug's production. When asked to explain the plummet in production, the UNDCP pointed to a new revolutionary government that had seized power in 1996 called the Taliban, a strict fundamentalist Muslim sect that imposed its will on the Afghanistan population.

The Taliban rulers were not popular, but many Afghans, weary of the prevailing lawlessness in many parts of the country, were delighted by the Taliban's successes in stamping out corruption, restoring peace, and allowing commerce to flourish again. In 1999, after many years of international pressure, Taliban leader Mullah Omar issued a total ban on opium poppy planting for the next season because growing a narcotic is a violation of Muslim law, which forbids any type of intoxication. In a *Vanity Fair* article, journalist Maureen Orth, who traveled widely in Afghanistan, reported, "The Taliban ban on poppy growing was the largest, most successful interdiction of drugs in history."

to show that they were serious in declaring a ban on opium production."[44]

Representatives of American military forces in Afghanistan share this view. While searching for Taliban fighters, which is their highest priority, U.S. soldiers routinely discover opium fields but are under orders not to destroy them. Journalist Tim McGirk, writing for *Time* magazine, quoted one American diplomat as saying, "The attitude is, 'Hey, it's not our problem.'"[45] U.S. military spokesman Sergeant Major Harrison Sarles acknowledges, "We're not a drug task force. That's not part of our mission. Drugs? What drugs?"[46]

American diplomats say that many of the local Afghan commanders upon whom they rely for political and military support are mixed up in the drug business. According to one American diplomat, "Without money from drugs, our friendly warlords can't pay their militias. It's as simple as that."[47]

The Uphill Battle Against Opium

In 2014 the United States will reach the centennial of its opium prohibition. Yet in spite of that law and the tens of billions of dollars spent annually attempting to stamp out the drug, America's cities remain awash in opium and an assortment of drugs derived from it. Regardless of America's commitment to eradicate this highly addictive narcotic, law enforcement agencies admit that the flow to America's streets has shown no sign of subsiding. Opium has been a remarkably resilient opponent in America's war on drugs.

Many responsible policy makers, law enforcement officers, and community leaders are frankly skeptical about winning the war on opium. Most experts studying America's history of opium use and abuse agree that past and current governmental policies to eradicate, confiscate, or otherwise eliminate the drug have failed and will continue to do so for a variety of reasons. Foremost in the minds of many is the colossal profit margin on opium. Joseph D. McNamara, the former chief of police of Kansas City, Missouri; Miami, Florida; and San Jose, California, explains:

> It's the money. After 33 years as a police officer in three of the country's largest cities, that is my message to the righteous politicians who obstinately proclaim that a war on drugs will lead to a drug-free America. About $500 of heroin or opium in a source country will bring in as much as $100,000 on the streets of an American city. All the cops, armies, prisons, and executions in the world cannot impede a market with that kind of tax-free profit-margin.[48]

Another explanation often cited for the failure to suppress opium is the ubiquitous criminal element. Author Martin Booth views the problem this way:

> The advantage in this terrible global game lies with the criminal. Just as the traffickers and dealers, the drug barons and smugglers manage to stay one step ahead of the enforcement officers chasing them. They will always

find a friendly bank, a compliant accountant, an underpaid official, or a receptive lawyer to assist them.[49]

Yet other experts recommend that consuming nations take a broader and more compassionate approach toward addressing economic development in poor opium-producing nations. Professor Barnett Rubin, director of studies for the Center for International Cooperation at New York University, suggests, "The fastest way to stop opium production is to enhance security and foster economic development. Nobody should be under the illusion that without security structures and economic development that the drug economy will be halted, or even significantly reduced."[50]

Efforts of Consumer Nations

Lee P. Brown, who served as President Bill Clinton's first director of the White House Office of National Drug Control Policy, blames America for its opium problem: "I'm not operating under any illusion that we will ever stop the growth of the opium poppy. What I'm saying is the best way to deal with the problem is not to use it. If we didn't use it in this country, it would be futile for the other countries to grow and try to satisfy a demand that does not exist."[51]

A class of fifth graders participates in a drug education program, one of many programs aimed at discouraging the use of narcotics.

American social institutions joined forces with law enforcement agencies in the 1970s to prevent the use of opium. Today, in addition to the federal government, organizations as diverse as churches and synagogues, schools and universities, youth organizations, national health organizations, police and sheriff departments, and organized sports programs have programs in place to discourage the use of opium.

Private and public agencies in the United States and other consumer nations conduct educational programs aimed at deterring drug use in general and opium and heroin use in particular. Most programs are aimed at schoolchildren, because studies conducted by health institutes indicate that they are most vulnerable to peer pressure to experiment with drugs. Programs such as the Drug Abuse Resistance Education (DARE) program send representatives to elementary and junior high schools to teach strategies for remaining drug free.

Among those who make suggestions or criticize government attempts is Peter G. Bourne, President Jimmy Carter's drug policy chief in 1977 and 1978, who plainly doubts the opium problem is solvable yet presents a realistic view of possibly controlling it: "There is no political mileage in saying we can't solve this problem. But I think the reality is that we cannot solve it in its entirety and that we have to accept that any measures we take are only going to be palliative"[52]

Facing an uphill battle, many Americans nonetheless believe the cost to wage the war is worth paying. Some want to see more money spent on law enforcement, others on treatment and prevention, while a minority wants to buy and destroy the entire crop before it is harvested. The issues are complicated because they span international borders, include large numbers of people, and involve conflicting moral values. Whatever path is taken, it is certain that the cost to contest opium trafficking will continue to be an issue for many years.

Notes

Chapter 1: A Strange and Mysterious Flower

1. Quoted in L.D. Kapoor, *Opium Poppy: Botany, Chemistry, and Pharmacology.* Binghamton, NY: Hawthorne, 1997, p. 5.
2. Quoted in Kapoor, *Opium Poppy*, p. 5.
3. Quoted in Martin Booth, *Opium: A History.* New York: St. Martin's, 1996, p. 17.
4. Quoted in Booth, *Opium: A History*, p. 24.
5. Quoted in Opioids, "Opium Pipe Smoker," 2001. www.opioids.com.
6. Quoted in Barbara Hodgson, *In the Arms of Morpheus: The Tragic History of Laudanum, Morphine, and Patient Medicines.* Buffalo, NY: Firefly, 2001, p. 9.
7. William Beal, "The Plant of Joy," 2001. www.opioids.com.
8. Quoted in Electronic Text Center, University of Virginia, "Samuel Taylor Coleridge: Kubla Khan." http://etext.lib.virginia.edu.
9. Quoted in Poppies Global, *"Papaver Somniferum: The Plant of Joy,"* 2003. www.poppiesglobal.com.
10. Quoted in Opioids, "Charles Baudelaire," 2001. www.opioids.com.
11. Quoted in Electronic Text Center, "Samuel Taylor Coleridge."
12. Quoted in Barbara Hodgson, *Opium: A Portrait of the Heavenly Demon.* San Francisco: Chronicle Books, 1999, p. 4.
13. Quoted in Hodgson, *In the Arms of Morpheus*, pp. 34–35.
14. Miriam Florence Leslie, "Tourists in an Opium Den," *San Francisco Memoirs,* www.sanfranciscomemoirs.com/stories.html.
15. Quoted in Hodgson, *In the Arms of Morpheus*, p. 14.

16. Quoted in Opioids, "Opium Pipe Smoker."
17. Quoted in Opioids, "Opium Pipe Smoker."

Chapter 2: The Search for Better Health

18. Quoted in Jesse Sublett, "Snake Oil Cures Turbulent Instinct," *Weekly Wire*, September 15, 1997. www.weekly wire.com.
19. Quoted in John Spenser Hill, "Opium and the 'Dream' of *Kubla Khan*," www.eiu.edu.
20. Solomon Snyder, *Drugs and the Brain*. New York: Scientific American, 1986, p. 205.

Chapter 3: The Opium Alliance

21. Quoted in Adrian Cowell, "The Opium Kings," February 1996. www.pbs.org.
22. Quoted in Cowell, "The Opium Kings."
23. Mark Corcoran, "Iran—the Golden Crescent," February 2001. www.abc.net.au.
24. Quoted in U.S. Department of Justice, "The Supply of Illicit Drugs to the United States," March 2004. www.usdoj.gov.
25. Alfred W. McCoy, "The Logistics of Opium," February 2004. www.drugtext.org.

Chapter 4: The Costs of America's Opium Problem

26. Quoted in Poppies Global, "*Papaver Somniferum*."
27. Booth, *Opium*, p. 209.
28. William Burroughs, "Letter from a Master Addict to Dangerous Drugs," *British Journal of Addiction*, August 3, 1956, p. 44.
29. Quoted in The Drug Library, "A Modern Opium Eater," 2002. www.druglibrary.org.
30. Quoted in Edward M. Brecher, "Opium Smoking Is Outlawed," 2002. www.druglibrary.org.

31. *Drug Abuse—Research Shows Treatment Is Effective, but Benefits May Be Overstated*. Washington, DC: General Accounting Office Report, April 27, 1998, p. 77.

Chapter 5: The International Politics of Opium

32. Quoted in Alfred W. McCoy, "Opium: Opium History, Basic Terms." www.opioids.com.

33. Quoted in Mark Berniker, "Afghanistan Stands on Brink of Becoming a Narco-State," *Eurasia Insight*, February 2004. www.eurasianet.org.

34. Quoted in Ron Moreau and Sami Yousafzai, "Flowers of Destruction," *Newsweek*, July 14, 2003, p. 38.

35. Quoted in *People's Daily*, "Thai Army Says Golden Triangle Opium Increasing Due to Afghan Ban," January 2002. www.fpeng.peopledaily.com.cn.

36. Quoted in U.S. Department of State, "International Narcotics Control Strategy Report," March 2002. www.state.gov.

37. Quoted in *People's Daily*, "Myanmar Launches Opium Eradication Project," May 2002. http://english.people daily.com.cn.

38. Quoted in Pierre-Arnoud Chouvy, "Ministerial Conference on the Drug Routes from Central Asia to Europe," May 2003. www.pa-chouvy.org.

39. Quoted in Berniker, "Afghanistan Stands on Brink."

40. Quoted in Berniker, "Afghanistan Stands on Brink."

41. UN Office on Drugs and Crime, "Opium Survey Afghanistan 2003," March 2004. www.unodc.org.

42. Alexander Cockburn and Jeffrey St. Clair, "Politics of a Bumper Crop: Opium and Afghanistan," *CounterPunch*, March 6, 2002. www.counterpunch.org.

43. Quoted in Info Imagination, "Abandoning Afghan Opium Eradication Effort," April 5, 2002. www.infoimagination.org.

44. Quoted in Info Imagination, "Abandoning Afghan Opium Eradication Effort."

45. Quoted in Tim McGirk, "Drugs, What Drugs?" *Time*, August 18, 2003, p. 18.

46. Quoted in McGirk, "Drugs, What Drugs?" p. 18.
47. Quoted in McGirk, "Drugs, What Drugs?" p. 19.
48. Quoted in Opioids, "Deady Shortcuts," 2002. www.opioids.com.
49. Booth, *Opium: A History*, p. 338.
50. Quoted in Berniker, "Afghanistan Stands on Brink."
51. Quoted in Cowell, "The Opium Kings."
52. Quoted in Cowell, "The Opium Kings."

Organizations to Contact

Drug Abuse Resistance Education (DARE)
9800 La Cienega Blvd., Suite 401
Inglewood, CA 90301
(800) 223-3273
www.dare.com

The DARE Web site provides young adults a variety of educational drug information and strategies for remaining drug free.

Narconon International
7060 Hollywood Blvd., Suite 220
Hollywood, CA 90028
(323) 962-2404
fax: (323) 962-6872
www.narconon.org

Narconon is a drug rehabilitation organization that specializes in opium addiction as well as other forms of addiction. The Web site provides factual information about opium and provides discussions about addiction and about the best approaches to help addicts.

National Institute on Drug Abuse (NIDA)
6001 Executive Blvd., Room 5213
Bethesda, MD 20892-9561
(301) 443-1124
www.drugabuse.gov

NIDA provides the latest information on opium and other abused drugs in the United States. The Web site contains research as well as statistics on opium use and focuses on warning the public of the risks involved with opium and other addictive drugs.

Office of National Drug Control Policy (ONDCP)
Drug Policy Information Clearinghouse
PO Box 6000
Rockville, MD 20849-6000
(800) 666-3332
www.whitehousedrugpolicy.gov

The principal purpose of the ONDCP is to establish policies, priorities, and objectives for the nation's drug control program. The goals of the program are to reduce illicit drug use, manufacturing, and trafficking, drug-related crime and violence, and drug-related health consequences.

Stop the Drug War
1623 Connecticut Ave. NW, 3rd Fl.
Washington, DC 20009
(202) 293-8340
http://stopthedrugwar.org

This organization was founded in 1993 and has grown into a major educational and advocacy organization and network of citizens working for reform of U.S. drug laws.

Teens in Prevention (TiP)
660 South Mesa Hills Dr., Suite 2000
El Paso, TX 79912
(915) 832-6233
www.deatip.net

Teens in Prevention is a youth-oriented, community-supported network of school-based organizations that focuses on individual responsibility, positive peer pressure, and community mobilization in hopes of reducing substance abuse and violence.

U.S. Department of State
2201 C St. NW
Washington, DC 20520
(202) 647-4000
www.state.gov

The U.S. Department of State is the American diplomatic agency responsible for maintaining a secure and democratic country. Its Web site contains links to thousands of current events of interest to the State Department as well as dozens of documents on America's war on drugs and specific cases dealing with the international opium trade.

U.S. Drug Enforcement Administration (DEA)
2401 Jefferson Davis Hwy.
Alexandria, VA 22301
(202) 307-7977
www.usdoj.gov/dea

The DEA is responsible for defining and enforcing all laws governing illegal drug use in America. Its Web site provides a broad range of information on illegal drugs in the United States. The site describes each illicit drug, discusses laws governing the drugs, and reports on government actions to curtail their entry and use in the United States.

For Further Reading

Thomas De Quincey, *Confessions of an English Opium Eater.* Oxford: Oxford University Press, 1821, reprinted in 1998. This book is considered a literary masterpiece because of its vivid and fascinating account of the pains and pleasures of opium use as well as an autobiographical account of De Quincey's youth.

Barbara Hodgson, *Opium: A Portrait of the Heavenly Demon.* San Francisco: Chronicle, 1999. This is a short yet beautiful book filled with photographs, sketches, paintings, engravings, and other artwork featuring opium-related scenes and paraphernalia. This book is an excellent starting point for understanding the history and effects of opium.

Dean Latimer and Jeff Goldberg, *Flowers in the Blood.* New York: Franklin Watts, 1981. The authors provide a history of opium, from its earliest uses through its medical phase and finally its use by addicts as a narcotic. This is one of the few books that explores possible cures for addiction.

Mark David Merlin, *On the Trail of the Ancient Opium Poppy.* London: Associated University Presses, 1984. Merlin's book is principally focused on archaeological evidence for the early use of opium by a variety of civilizations. It is well written, illustrated, and documented.

Pam Walker and Elaine Wood, *Narcotics.* San Diego: Lucent, 2004. Discusses the uses and abuses of opium, morphine, and heroin from ancient times until today. Includes chapters about addiction, treatment, and the efforts of law enforcement to stamp out narcotics.

Works Consulted

Books

Martin Booth, *Opium: A History*. New York: St. Martin's, 1996. Booth traces opium's history, from the first evidence of poppy cultivation through the drug wars of today. He explores opium's uses in different cultures, its international political implications, and its horrifying ramifications for addicts.

David T. Courtwright, *Dark Paradise: A History of Opiate Addiction in America*. Cambridge, MA: Harvard University Press, 2001. This book investigates opiate use in America from the mid-1800s to the present day. The author explores the early use of opiates in medicine, complications of addiction, and what he views as the failure of government strategies to stop the flow of opiates into America.

Drug Abuse—Research Shows Treatment Is Effective, but Benefits May Be Overstated. Washington, DC: General Accounting Office Report, April 27, 1998. This government publication independently evaluates the effectiveness of drug treatment programs and verifies the results of studies it reviews.

Drug Control—Long-Standing Problems Hinder U.S. International Efforts. Washington, DC: General Accounting Office Report, February 27, 1998. This is a government publication containing testimony during hearings of the Subcommittee on National Security.

Barbara Hodgson, *In the Arms of Morpheus: The Tragic History of Laudanum, Morphine, and Patient Medicines*. Buffalo, NY: Firefly, 2001. The author provides a disturbing story of how a simple but mystical substance, touted as a miracle drug, enslaved unwitting generations of nineteenth-century writers, artists, and ordinary citizens. Hodgson recounts how opium was welcomed into the homes of rich and poor alike under the guise of medicinal uses and later as morphine.

L.D. Kapoor, *Opium Poppy: Botany, Chemistry, and Pharmacology*. Binghamton, NY: Hawthorne, 1997. This book is a comprehensive resource that explores the opium poppy's origin, distribution, chemistry, and uses and abuses from ancient civilizations through the present. It covers crop production and explores the chemical and pharmaceutical by-products of the poppy.

Alfred W. McCoy, *The Politics of Heroin: CIA Complicity in the Global Drug Trade*. New York: Lawrence Hill, 2003. McCoy asserts that the Central Intelligence Agency has been actively involved in the global trafficking of opium and heroin. The author documents what he perceives to be dishonesty and illegal dealings at the highest levels of American government. The final chapter documents recent U.S. involvement in the narcotics trade in Afghanistan and Pakistan before and after the fall of the Taliban in 2002.

Solomon Snyder, *Drugs and the Brain*. New York: Scientific American, 1986. This book provides a history of drug use and pharmacology research. It is well illustrated and organized by the major classes of drugs. The book also gives an excellent history of opium use over the past two centuries.

Periodicals

William Burroughs, "Letter from a Master Addict to Dangerous Drugs," *British Journal of Addiction*, August 3, 1956.

Tim McGirk, "Drugs, What Drugs?" *Time*, August 18, 2003.

Ron Moreau and Sami Yousafzai, "Flowers of Destruction," *Newsweek*, July 14, 2003.

Maureen Orth, "Afghanistan's Deadly Habit," *Vanity Fair*, March 2002.

Internet Sources

William Beal, "The Plant of Joy," 2001. www.opioids.com.

Mark Berniker, "Afghanistan Stands on Brink of Becoming a Narco-State," *Eurasia Insight,* February 2004. www.eurasianet.org.

Edward M. Brecher, *The Consumers Union Report on Licit and Illicit Drugs,* 2002. www.druglibrary.org.

———, "Opiates for Pain Relief, for Tranquilization, and for Pleasure," 2002. www.druglibrary.org.

———, "Opium Smoking Is Outlawed," 2002. www.druglibrary.org.

Pierre-Arnoud Chouvy, "Ministerial Conference on the Drug Routes from Central Asia to Europe," May 2003. www.pa-chouvy.org.

Alexander Cockburn and Jeffrey St. Clair, "Politics of a Bumper Crop: Opium and Afghanistan," *CounterPunch,* March 6, 2002. www.counterpunch.org.

Mark Corcoran, "Iran—the Golden Crescent," February 2001. www.abc.net.au.

Adrian Cowell, "The Opium Kings," February 1996. www.pbs.org.

Gretchen Dickey, "Downtown Opium Dens Attracted Many," www.epcc.edu.

The Drug Library, "A Modern Opium Eater," 2002. www.druglibrary.org.

———, "An Opium-Eater in America," www.druglibrary.org.

Electronic Text Center, University of Virginia, "Samuel Taylor Coleridge: Kubla Khan." http://etext.lib.virginia.edu.

John Spenser Hill, "Opium and the 'Dream' of *Kubla Khan,*" www.eiu.edu.

Steve Hirsch, "Officials, Critics Clash over Myanmar Opium Questions," *U.N. Wire,* 2003. www.unwire.org.

Info Imagination, "Abandoning Afghan Opium Eradication Effort," April 5, 2002. www.infoimagination.org.

Miriam Florence Leslie, "Tourists in an Opium Den," *San Francisco Memoirs,* www.sanfranciscomemoirs.com/stories.html.

Alfred W. McCoy, "The Logistics of Opium," February 2004. www.drugtext.org.

———, "Opium: Opium History, Basic Terms," www.opioids.com.

Andrew North, "The Drug Threat to Afghanistan," February 2004. http://news.bbc.co.uk.

Opioids, "Charles Baudelaire," 2001. www.opioids.com.

———, "Deadly Shortcuts," 2002. www.opioids.com.

———, "Opium Pipe Smoker," 2001. www.opioids.com.

People's Daily, "Myanmar Launches Opium Eradication Project," May 2002. http://english.peopledaily.com.cn.

———, "Thai Army Says Golden Triangle Opium Increasing Due to Afghan Ban," January 2002. www.fpeng.peopledaily.com.cn.

Poppies Global, "*Papaver Somniferum:* The Plant of Joy," 2003. www.poppiesglobal.com.

Jesse Sublett, "Snake Oil Cures Turbulent Instinct," *Weekly Wire*, September 15, 1997. www.weeklywire.com.

UN Office on Drugs and Crime, "Opium Survey Afghanistan 2003," March 2004. www.unodc.org.

U.S. Department of Justice, "The Supply of Illicit Drugs to the United States," March 2004. www.usdoj.gov.

U.S. Department of State, "International Narcotics Control Strategy Report," 2001. www.state.gov.

———, "International Narcotics Control Strategy Report," March 2002. www.state.gov.

Mark Wightman, "Breakthrough? Study Finds Dopamine Cannot Be Source of Pleasure in Brain," 1999. www.unc.edu.

Web Sites

The Drug Library (www.druglibrary.org). This is a comprehensive online library dedicated to providing information about licit and illicit drugs. The library includes medical descriptions of drugs, their histories, dangers, and U.S. laws governing their use.

Opioids (www.opioids.com). This site provides a comprehensive discussion of opium's history, use, effects on users, and laws and detailed scientific information. In addition to its accuracy representing opium, it also includes writers who advocate the legalization of opium.

Public Broadcasting Station (www.pbs.org). The Public Broadcasting Station created a Web site for a comprehensive television program called *The Opium Kings: Opium Throughout
History*. It includes opium's history, cultivation, distribution by
crime cartels, attempts by law enforcement to eradicate it, and
its worldwide popularity.

Index

Picture Credits

About the Author

James Barter received his undergraduate degree in history and classics at the University of California at Berkeley, followed by graduate studies in ancient history and archaeology at the University of Pennsylvania. Mr. Barter has taught history as well as Latin and Greek.

A Fulbright scholar at the American Academy in Rome, Mr. Barter worked on archaeological sites in and around the city as well as on sites in the Naples area. He has also worked and traveled extensively in Greece.

Mr. Barter resides in Rancho Santa Fe, California, and lectures throughout the San Diego area.